IF I HAD A HAMMER

Stories of Building Homes and Hope
with Habitat for Humanity

DAVID RUBEL

with a foreword by
Jimmy Carter

An Agincourt Press Book

CANDLEWICK PRESS

An Agincourt Press Book
President: David Rubel
Senior Editor: Julia Rubel
Design: Jon Glick/mouse+tiger design

First paperback edition 2010

The Library of Congress has cataloged the hardcover edition as follows:

Rubel, David.
If I had a hammer : stories of building homes and hope with Habitat for Humanity / David Rubel.
—1st ed.
p.   cm.
ISBN 978-0-7636-4701-8 (hardcover)
1. Habitat for Humanity International, Inc. 2. Low-income housing.
3. Housing—Religious aspects—Christianity—Societies, etc.   I. Title.
HV97.H32R83 2009
363.5'83—dc22   2009025691

ISBN 978-0-7636-4769-8 (paperback)

10 11 12 13 14 15 CCP 10 9 8 7 6 5 4 3 2 1

Printed in Shenzhen, Guangdong, China

This book was typeset in Adobe Caslon Pro and Clearface Gothic.

Candlewick Press
99 Dover Street
Somerville, Massachusetts 02144

visit us at www.candlewick.com

Contents

Foreword

by Jimmy Carter

WHEN I LEFT THE WHITE HOUSE, retired by the results of the 1980 election, I didn't know what I was going to do next. I knew that I had a life expectancy of twenty-five more years, and I wondered how I could capitalize on the experience and knowledge of having been the leader of the greatest nation in the world. Looking to my Christian faith for a way forward, I began teaching Sunday school again at Maranatha Baptist Church—where my wife, Rosalynn, and I attend services in our hometown of Plains, Georgia.

Our religious beliefs are important to us. I have taught Sunday school since I was a teen, and we attend services regularly, but for a time that had been the extent of it. Like many people, Rosalynn and I have searched to find an outlet to put that faith into action. Rarely have we found the opportunity to follow Jesus Christ's example of reaching out to those who are poor and in need and treating them as equals.

The underlying problem is that sometimes it is difficult for people like us—who have homes, good educations, and fruitful careers—to cross the chasm that separates us from people who may have none of these blessings. Often, the needy are scorned by us more affluent people who think to ourselves, *Well, if those poor people would only work as hard as I do or study as hard as I do, then they could provide a good home for their families, just as I do.* That kind of prejudice can be difficult to overcome.

Fortunately for Rosalynn and me, the international headquarters of Habitat for Humanity was located in Americus, Georgia, just nine miles from Plains. In Habitat's work, building homes for those in need, we saw the opportunity—as so many others have—to put our faith into practice.

The goal of Habitat for Humanity is to rid the world of substandard, or poverty, housing. Habitat works hard to do this by building simple homes in partnership with families in need. These partner families pay the full cost of their new homes over time through no-profit loans that Habitat grants them. The prices of Habitat homes remain affordable because the homes aren't extravagant and because they're built with volunteer labor, including the labor of the partner families.

THERE'S NO WAY to describe exactly why Habitat means so much to me, but I will try. If you are a person of faith, you learn certain basic lessons about truth, justice, love, and sharing that shape your life. It doesn't matter whether you learn these lessons in a church (as I did), in a synagogue, in a mosque, or in a temple. Wherever the lessons are learned, they remain largely the same. One is that people who have been blessed with wealth should share that wealth with others who are in need. Finding a way to do this, however, can be hard because of the divide that separates the rich and the poor.

People tend to feel most comfortable with those just like themselves—people who have the same skin color, who talk like us, who live in equally nice homes—so we often shut out others who are different. It's not easy to break through the barriers that we naturally erect. The great gift of Habitat for Humanity is that it offers us a way to reach out to fellow humans who don't have a decent place in which to live. In fact, it's the best way that I know to live out the highest moral values of my faith, because Habitat sees decent housing as a human right.

Human rights can be defined in many different ways. If you ask Americans on the street to name some human rights, they are likely to say freedom of speech, freedom of religion, the right to assemble, the right to a trial by jury, or the right to elect one's leaders. Those are perfectly good *legal* human rights. But one of the most important—a human right that people often forget—is the right to lead a good life. By this I mean the right to have food to eat, a place to sleep at night, access to doctors and education, and a decent job, as well as self-respect and dignity.

We affluent Americans frequently fail to realize that these things are missing from the lives of many people, not only around the world but also here in our own country. When the new millennium began in 2000, I was asked to make a few speeches in different places around the world about the greatest challenge facing humanity. It didn't take me long to identify what that challenge was: the growing separation between rich and poor. Did you know that in the year 1900, the people who lived in the world's ten richest countries were, on average, about nine times richer than the people who lived in the world's ten poorest countries? That doesn't seem like a lot, but as time passed, the gap widened. By 1960, the world's richest people were thirty times wealthier than the world's poorest people, and today the world's richest people are more than seventy-five times more wealthy!

Rosalynn and Jimmy Carter inspect a wall during the 2008 Carter Work Project in Mississippi.

Even worse, there are many more poor people than most of us realize. Over half of the world's six billion people live on less than two dollars a day. Over a billion people live on less than one dollar a day. Imagine how you might live on just one dollar a day, and you can get some idea of their plight. That one dollar a day would have to pay for food, shelter, and clothing; and even if it did, which isn't likely, you would have nothing left over for education, health care, or the future. Not surprisingly, most people who earn only a few dollars a day don't eat well and are forced to live in slums. Even in America, the wealthiest nation in the world, nearly one in three people lives in a house that neither you nor I would consider a fit place to live.

Habitat makes it possible for us to work side by side with partner families and help them improve their lives so that they can not just survive but thrive in the world. Helping a family in need move into a home is the primary mission of Habitat for Humanity. Yet, because of the unique way in which Habitat operates, the organization accomplishes much more. It brings together people of different backgrounds and stations in life to create an environment in which everyone is equal.

I've learned that these new homeowners are just as hardworking and ambitious as I am, their family values are just as good as mine, and they want the same things for themselves and their children as I want for me and mine. What Rosalynn and I have seen time and again is that when people become homeowners, their dignity and self-respect increase dramatically. Because they've worked so hard themselves to complete the home, they become filled with a new pride that inspires them to reach for other things that they previously considered out of their grasp, such as an education.

We know this because we often revisit Habitat sites where we have built in the past in order to see what has happened to the homes and the neighborhoods. Never have we seen a Habitat home with graffiti on the walls or a broken windowpane that wasn't repaired or a lawn that wasn't mowed. People who build and pay for their own homes are proud of what they have accomplished, and they don't let their homes deteriorate.

You can see this pride in the faces of the partner families on the day that they receive the keys to their new home. They know that they aren't being given a handout but a hand up, because they have done their share of the work and they will be paying their share of the cost. Participating in this ceremony, especially when you have helped in constructing the house, can be an overwhelming, emotional experience.

THERE IS NO QUESTION that helping to create a decent home for a partner family is a significant act of giving, but volunteers typically find that they receive something in return that is even more valuable: a feeling of satisfaction and a connection to other people. Knowing that you have worked alongside other volunteers to change a family's life is a powerful feeling that you will want to experience again and again. For this reason, Habitat volunteers keep coming back to work on Habitat projects.

Rosalynn and I began working regularly on Habitat job sites in 1984, when we arranged for a group of forty-two of our friends to travel to New York City for a weeklong project rebuilding an apartment house on the Lower East Side. Since then, we have spent one week every year leading a work project either here in the United States or in a foreign country such as South Africa, Hungary, or the Philippines. We haven't missed a year yet, and we expect to continue as long as we are able.

One reason is the way the work makes us feel. In all of our lives, there are usually a few precious moments when we feel exalted—that is, when we reach above our normal level of existence to a higher plane of excitement and achievement.

I remember feeling that way when Rosalynn agreed to marry me and when our children were born. Taking the oath of office as president of the United States was another moment of exaltation for me, as was seeing the fruition of the time I spent negotiating a peace treaty between Israel and Egypt, not a word of which has been broken to this day. When I went to the army hospital in Germany where the hostages that had been taken in Iran were being treated after their release, I was nervous because I didn't know how they would receive me. But when they all stood up and cheered as I walked into the room and then embraced me one by one with tears in their eyes, I felt exalted.

It may surprise you, but I also experience a feeling of exaltation at the end of each Habitat work project, when I give a Bible as a gift to the new homeowners, along with the keys to their new house. My heart and soul always are exalted, and sometimes tears of joy run down my face.

I predict that every one of you who volunteers to help others in need will feel this same sense of exaltation. I believe that, in making what seems to be a sacrifice, you will find fulfillment in the memorable experience of helping others less fortunate than yourself.

When you pay your own way to a Habitat job site in a distant land and furnish your own tools, and you're working hard and getting up early, you can sometimes think to yourself, *This is a big sacrifice I'm making for the folks who are going to live in this house.* But what you'll find is that the "sacrifice" actually is a blessing. I know this because I've learned the secret that so many other Habitat volunteers have learned: you always get much more out of the work than you put in.

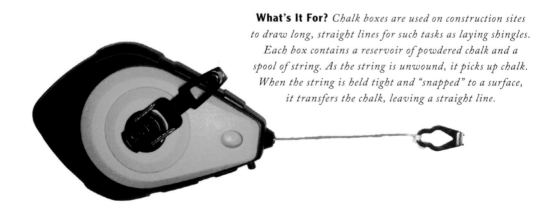

What's It For? *Chalk boxes are used on construction sites to draw long, straight lines for such tasks as laying shingles. Each box contains a reservoir of powdered chalk and a spool of string. As the string is unwound, it picks up chalk. When the string is held tight and "snapped" to a surface, it transfers the chalk, leaving a straight line.*

At age four

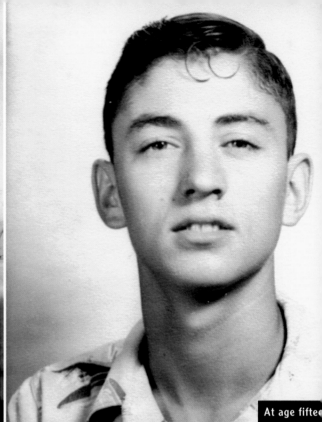

At age fifteen

At Koinonia Farm

With Jimmy Carter

1. In the Beginning

WHEN MILLARD FULLER WAS A BOY growing up in the Alabama countryside, his father gave him a young pig to raise. Millard fattened the pig and sold it for a good price. Then he used the money he earned to buy and raise more young pigs, which he also fattened and sold.

It didn't take Millard long to realize that he liked money; and as he got older, he thought up more and better ways of making it. In college and in law school, he ran a number of businesses that often competed with his schoolwork. One involved delivering cakes to fellow students on their birthdays. Another involved the purchase of a vacant lot onto which Millard and a partner moved an old army barrack. They made a great deal of money renting out rooms in the building to students who needed an inexpensive place to live.

By the time Millard Fuller graduated from law school in 1960, he was already well on his way to becoming a millionaire. He started a law practice but didn't practice much law. Instead, he and

SNAPSHOTS FROM THE LIFE OF HABITAT FOR HUMANITY FOUNDER MILLARD FULLER

1

his partner ran a mail-order company, selling a wide variety of goods, from tractor cushions to doormats to cookbooks. Fuller was successful because he had a lot of ideas and was adaptable. He also had great charm as a salesman.

With so much money pouring in, Fuller bought a fancy home for his wife and children in Montgomery, Alabama, and a second home on a lake, complete with two speedboats. To most people, it seemed as though he was living a dream life. But to Fuller, the dream was becoming a nightmare.

The first warning signs were health problems. During the early 1960s, Fuller began experiencing pain in his neck and back that wouldn't go away. Sometimes he also found himself gasping for air, unable to catch his breath. He ignored these symptoms, which were probably caused by stress, and went on making money until one day in November 1965 his wife, Linda, told him that she was leaving him. The reason, she said, was his obsession with his business. He worked so long and so hard that he never had any time for her or their children. The next day, Linda Fuller traveled to New York City to seek advice from a minister she knew there.

Linda's departure left Millard feeling confused and empty. But rather than simply feel sorry for himself, he decided to act. He followed Linda to New York and told her that he wanted to save their marriage. They talked for a while about what changes they needed to make. In the end, they decided that the only way to solve their problems would be to give away their money, so they did just that. Their friends thought they were crazy, but in Millard's words, "We had gone too far down the wrong road to be able to correct our direction with a slight detour. We simply had to go back and start all over again, but this time we would let God choose the road for us."

Clarence Jordan inspects a crop at Koinonia Farm.

A<small>FTER DONATING</small> all their wealth to charity, the Fullers felt so happy that they decided to celebrate with a family trip to Florida. On their way back to Montgomery, they stopped in southwestern Georgia to visit two of Millard's friends who were living at a place called Koinonia Farm. The plan was to stay only a few hours; instead, the Fullers remained at Koinonia for more than a month.

Located not far from Americus, Georgia, Koinonia Farm is an experimental Christian community that was started in 1942 to test the social theories of its principal founder, Clarence Jordan. An ordained Baptist minister, Jordan was also a scholar in the field of Koine Greek, the original language of the New Testament. (As opposed to the Old Testament, also known as the Hebrew Bible, the New Testament begins with the four Gospels, which tell the story of the life of Jesus Christ. It also contains the Acts of the Apostles, a later section that describes the activities of the early Christians following Jesus's death.) The Greek word *koinonia,* which appears frequently in the New Testament, refers to the ideals of fellowship and sharing that Jesus preached.

Jordan believed that in the two thousand years since Jesus's death, Christian churches had become too weighed down with

Members of the Koinonia community gather on a farm truck during the 1940s or 1950s.

ritual. At Koinonia, he wanted to get back to the original teachings
of Jesus as presented in the Gospels. Specifically, he wanted to
re-create the lifestyle of the earliest Christians as described in the
Acts of the Apostles. The families who joined Jordan at Koinonia
lived together, ate together, worked together, studied the Bible
together, and shared all of their possessions with one another—just
as the early Christians had.

According to Jordan, nothing mattered more than following
the example set by Jesus, especially with regard to loving all people
and caring for the poor. This approach to life got Jordan into
trouble, however, because in the white-dominated South of the 1940s,
1950s, and 1960s, *all people* didn't include blacks. Because the white
members of the Koinonia community treated African Americans as

equals, they were threatened by white neighbors, economically as well as physically. Most businesses in Sumter County (the Georgia county in which Koinonia is located) refused to sell the Koinonians farm supplies, nor would they buy Koinonia produce. As racial tensions increased, the Ku Klux Klan, which was strong in Sumter County, threatened to burn the farm down (and even tried to do so from time to time). Despite these hardships, the Koinonians refused to give up, and they managed to survive by developing a mail-order business, which allowed them to ship the pecans that they grew to buyers outside Sumter County.

When Millard Fuller first arrived at Koinonia in December 1965, he was searching for a new purpose to give meaning to his life. Having just given up the pursuit of money, he needed a new way to channel his considerable energy and drive. In Clarence Jordan, he found a friendly mentor. "God led me to Clarence in my hour of greatest need," Fuller said later. "[He] nurtured me back to emotional and spiritual health."

Koinonia Farm residents in a 1940s snapshot

M OST OF ALL, Fuller listened carefully as Jordan described his dislike for Christians who focused on prettifying their churches rather than helping the poor. Jordan referred to these people as Kleenex Christians because they wept for the poor in church but never did anything to help them.

When Fuller left Koinonia in January 1966, he tried to put Jordan's ideas into action by taking a job with Tougaloo College, an historically black school in Jackson, Mississippi. Fuller's assignment was to raise money for the school, and he worked out of Tougaloo's development office in New York City—a most unusual job choice for a white southerner in 1960s America.

Because of his intelligence, his liveliness, and his likable personality, Fuller performed well in his new job. But by early 1968, he was ready for something bigger, so he sent a note to Clarence Jordan. "I have just resigned my job with Tougaloo," the note read. "What have you got up your sleeve?" Jordan's reply was immediate: "Maybe God has something up His sleeve for both of us."

Clarence Jordan (left) and Millard Fuller at Koinonia Farm

Fuller returned to Koinonia and spent the next five years helping Jordan revitalize the now dwindling community. The centerpiece of their effort was the creation of Koinonia Partners, a series of "partnership ministries" that were designed to follow the example of Jesus by helping the poor of Sumter County. "Partnership farming" allowed low-income neighbors to farm Koinonia land free of rent. "Partnership industries" put people who needed jobs to work in the farm's fruitcake bakery, candy kitchen, pecan-shelling plant, and mail-order warehouse. "Partnership housing" used volunteer labor to build simple, decent houses for people who were living in run-down shacks without any toilets or running water. The money to pay for these ministries came from a new Fund for Humanity, which was supported by donations from people who believed in the principles practiced at Koinonia.

Volunteers complete a Koinonia Partners house in 1970.

When Jordan died in October 1969, Fuller took over leadership of Koinonia Farm and pressed ahead with the partnership ministries, of which the housing ministry was becoming by far the most important. Fuller quickly realized that he could build simple, decent houses for a very low price as long as the labor used to build those homes was volunteer. Using money donated to the Fund for Humanity, he bought enough construction materials to build several homes. Then he sold the homes to families who had taken part in their construction. None of the families could afford to repay the entire cost of the new house all at once, nor could they get loans from local banks, so Fuller offered them no-interest loans with monthly payments. The loans, known as mortgages in the real estate industry, had a term of twenty years.

The math was simple: Twenty years of monthly payments meant 240 payments in all. If the cost of a house was six thousand dollars, then a family could own that house for a monthly payment of just twenty-five dollars.

Fuller also realized that the housing program could become self-supporting. The monthly payments that homeowners made would replenish the Fund for Humanity, allowing Koinonia Partners to build more new homes. In this way, Fuller was able to build twenty-seven homes in less than five years—an enormous success beyond anyone's expectations. This achievement got Fuller thinking about new possibilities, and he was already in the mood for a change when the Disciples of Christ church contacted him in 1973, offering the opportunity to head a community development project in Zaire (an East African country now known as the Democratic Republic of the Congo). Millard and Linda jumped at the chance.

The Fullers and their four children spent the next three years

Millard and Linda Fuller with their children at Koinonia Farm in 1971

in Mbandaka, a city on the Congo River, where they oversaw the construction of nearly one hundred homes. These houses, which filled an empty field in the center of the extremely poor city, cost just two thousand dollars each to build. They were made of cement blocks produced at a

Millard Fuller reviews housing plans with a local man in Mbandaka, Zaire, in 1974.

block-making factory that the Fullers had also established. By the time the Fullers returned to America in the summer of 1976, Millard had a new obsession: ridding the world of poverty housing.

Fuller was sure that his program would work. Its elements were: collect donations in order to buy materials, build with volunteer labor, work in partnership with the future homeowners, sell the houses at no profit, and recycle the monthly payments into new home construction. In his head and in his heart, Fuller believed that this idea could save the world.

In September 1976, within weeks of his return from Zaire, Fuller invited a group of friends to join him for a weekend at Koinonia so that they could help him figure out what to do next. Over three days, twenty-seven people "prayed and dreamed and discussed and brainstormed together," according to Fuller. The central question they posed was, *What is God calling us to do with this idea?* In the end, they decided that God wanted them to form a new organization, which they called Habitat for Humanity.

In 1983, Habitat supporters walked seven hundred miles from Americus to Indianapolis, Indiana, in order to raise both funds and people's awareness of the organization.

Fuller's first move after the conference was to open a headquarters for Habitat in the back room of his new law office in Americus. At the same time, he returned to one of the core principles that he had learned from Clarence Jordan: The "haves" and the "have-nots" of the world are bound together. According to Jordan, the rich and the poor need each other. The poor need resources, such as money, in order to improve their lives; and the rich need a connection to God and other people, which their money can't buy. For this reason, Jordan saw the Fund for Humanity as an effective and dignified way to bring rich and poor together for the benefit of both. As Jordan once wrote, "What the poor need is not charity but capital, not caseworkers but coworkers. And what the rich need is a wise, honorable, and just way of divesting themselves of their overabundance."

Having already given away his own wealth and benefited from the experience, Fuller recognized the truth of Jordan's words and set about persuading other affluent people to support his new cause. Underlying this work was the assumption that human beings were inherently good. They just needed a way to let that goodness out.

WHEN JIMMY CARTER LEFT the White House after losing the 1980 election to Ronald Reagan, he returned to his family farm in Plains, Georgia, just nine miles west of Americus. The farm stands on land that the Carter family has owned since 1833, testifying to its deep roots in Sumter County. The former president's main project was the creation of the Carter Center in Atlanta to continue the work of promoting human rights and relieving human suffering that he had begun as president. But he wanted to do more.

"While I was still in Washington, during my last few weeks in the White House after the election, I picked up a copy of my hometown newspaper, the *Americus Times-Recorder,* hoping to find some solace," President Carter remembers. "Instead, I found a condemnation of me from Millard Fuller, because he had sent me an invitation to the dedication of some homes and I hadn't responded. At that time, I was getting forty thousand letters a day, and I never saw Millard's letter. But I did see his diatribe was condemning me for not caring about poor people. I had never heard of Habitat before, and I didn't know who this nut from my hometown was, but my first impression was negative."

President Carter and his wife, Rosalynn, began to get a different impression after they moved back to Plains and began attending Maranatha Baptist Church. "I was teaching Sunday school there," President Carter continues, "and a lot of Habitat volunteers would come over to hear me teach because I was just out of the White House then. They began to tell me more about Habitat and what it meant; and eventually, because of their intercession, I decided to invite Millard and Linda over to my house to meet with Rosalynn and me."

The first meeting between the Carters and the Fullers took place in early 1984. As Millard Fuller told the story, the conversation was rather brief, but it ended on a positive note, with Fuller asking the Carters, "Are you interested in Habitat for Humanity, or are you very interested?" and the president replying, "We're very interested." The Carters then suggested that Fuller send them a list of specific ways in which they could be of help.

The letter that Fuller sent to the Carters about a week later contained fifteen suggestions. These included serving on the Habitat board of directors, signing fund-raising letters, giving money themselves, volunteering to work on job sites, making public appearances on behalf of Habitat, and praying for the success of the organization. "I told Millard, 'Okay, I'll do two things,'" the president recalls with his trademark smile. "But eventually Rosalynn and I did all fifteen."

"Millard Fuller was the most charismatic, persuasive person I have ever known," Mrs. Carter agrees. "He talked us into every single one of those things."

By this time, Habitat headquarters had moved from Fuller's law office into its own building in Americus, but its operations were still quite small. When President Carter joined the board of directors in 1984, the organization had only seven employees. These people worked with about forty volunteers to oversee the activities of thirty-three affiliates in the United States and eighteen affiliates in other countries. (Affiliates are local groups that associate themselves with the international organization.) These affiliates had so far built or renovated 523 homes, most of them overseas.

Two things in particular were holding Habitat back: one was a lack of money, and the other was a lack of name recognition. President Carter was able to help with both problems immediately. Soon after joining the board of directors, he agreed to chair a two-year, ten-million-dollar fund drive that actually raised twelve million dollars. Even more important, in September 1984 he took part in the first Jimmy Carter Work Project (an annual event now known as the Jimmy and Rosalynn Carter Work Project). Although Habitat had been in operation for eight years at that point, few Americans had heard of it or knew anything about its activities. President Carter's willingness to pick up a hammer, however, quickly changed all of that.

DURING THE MID-1970S, a midtown Manhattan church called Metro Baptist began sponsoring a mission in a needy neighborhood of New York City known as Alphabet City because its principal streets are Avenues A, B, C, and D. This mission, the Graffiti Ministry Center on East Seventh Street between Avenues

The Mascot Flats apartment building as it appeared in 1984

B and C, became an oasis amid the drugs and crime that plagued the neighborhood.

Several years later, twenty-two-year-old Rob DeRocker, recently graduated from New York University, began attending Metro Baptist Church. Occasionally, he would hear reports from the minister running the Graffiti Ministry Center. "He was seeing people who were coming to his nighttime Bible classes and then going home to tenements where the rats were biting their children and there was no heat or hot water during the wintertime," Rob recalls. "He really wanted to do something about the problem, so he contacted Habitat for Humanity in Georgia. This was 1981 or so, before Jimmy Carter became involved, and Habitat was still quite small. Anyway, the Habitat board told the church to get its act together, raise money, and start an affiliate.

"For the next two years," Rob continues, "we sat around and prayed about having a Habitat project. Finally, everyone looked to me, maybe because I was the youngest person in the room, to do what was necessary to get a project launched. I said, 'Okay, I'll do it. But I don't know anything about housing, and I don't know anything about fund-raising.' Really, I didn't know anything about anything, and so I told the Lord the project would be a miserable failure and He would regret having made this move."

But Rob brought a great deal of energy to the project, and he learned most of what he needed to know as he went along. Soon, he began negotiating with the city for the purchase of a six-story building at 742 East Sixth Street between Avenues C and D. Once a respectable apartment house known as the Mascot Flats, it had since been abandoned and picked over by looters searching for building materials that they could resell. Several fires, some started accidentally and some set on purpose, had further gutted the building's interior.

The task of renovating the Mascot Flats soon turned out to be more than the new Habitat affiliate could handle. It required enormous amounts of money and manpower that Rob didn't have, and so progress was frustratingly slow. Then one day in March 1984, Rob read in the *New York Daily News* that Jimmy Carter was coming to New York City several weeks later to take part in an anniversary celebration for his friend Archbishop Iakovos, the head of the Greek Orthodox Church in North America. Sensing an opportunity, Rob wrote to Millard Fuller, asking whether Fuller would use his influence to persuade President Carter to visit the Mascot Flats job site.

Because Rob didn't expect much to come of his letter, he was shocked when Fuller woke him up with a phone call at seven in the morning. "Rob, what are you doin' in bed?" Fuller demanded. "I wasn't in bed, Millard. I was on my knees praying," a groggy Rob replied. "Yeah, right, your voice sounds like it," Fuller went on. "Get up, brother! We're not going to build houses in bed! And I've got news for you. President Carter's going to stop by your project."

On April 1, 1984, Rob DeRocker walked into the Waldorf Astoria Hotel and took the elevator up to the presidential suite. "I had just turned twenty-five," Rob says, "and I had never been in the presence of anyone of that stature before. So waiting outside the presidential suite at the Waldorf, I felt as though someone had stuck a vacuum cleaner hose into my mouth and sucked out all the moisture. Then, suddenly, there he was."

Rob then traveled with the president down to Alphabet City, where they toured the Mascot Flats. "There was no way to get to the top floor of that building without being a monkey," Rob explains, "because drug addicts had long ago taken apart the original staircase so they could sell its marble treads. The day before President Carter's visit, some volunteers had put up a wooden staircase, but it was pretty rickety and that made the Secret Service agents go nuts when the president started climbing it. He did climb it, though, and when he got to the roof of the building, he looked south toward the World Trade Center and Wall Street. Then he looked north toward the skyline of midtown Manhattan. Finally, he looked down over the edge of the roof into the vacant lot below, and amid all the rubble he saw an elderly woman cooking some food over an open fire. He was really moved by that, and when we got back down to the street, just as he was getting in his car, he said, 'Rob, Millard Fuller is my boss. If there's anything I can do to help you here, just let him know.' I sputtered out, 'Well, you know, Mr. President, maybe you could send a few carpenters from your church up here to help us.' I never, ever, ever thought he would be interested in coming himself. He said, 'We'll think about it.'"

President Carter did more than think about Rob's request. A day later, he called Millard Fuller and told him that he planned to put together a group of volunteers from Maranatha Baptist Church and that he would join them for the trip to New York City. "Of course," Rob says, "that changed everything."

Jimmy Carter already knew well how to use a hammer. As a boy in Plains, he had learned the basics of carpentry as a member of the Future Farmers of America, which taught him not only how to build houses but also how to make furniture, weld, and even do a little

Millard Fuller exhorts volunteers as they prepare to set off from Americus for the first Jimmy Carter Work Project.

blacksmithing. Because of this background, he knew how difficult renovating the Mascot Flats would be.

Initially, he worried that there wouldn't be enough interest to fill the eight-seat Habitat van, but soon he had a busload of volunteers. In all, forty-two traveled with the president to New York City on a chartered Trailways bus; and when they arrived, the local and national press were waiting for them. "All week long I've been getting calls from press people asking, 'Is President Carter really going to ride up on that bus? Is he really going to work in that building?'" Millard Fuller told a *New York Times* reporter. "I kept saying, 'Yes, and he's even going to sleep with us in the church dormitory.'"

As he had during his presidency, Jimmy Carter carried his own luggage; and when he walked into the men's dormitory of the Metro Baptist Church, he lifted his blue suitcase onto one of the top bunks. A Secret Service agent took the bunk beneath him. The next day, President Carter carried his own tools down to the job site, where he and the other volunteers worked alongside future homeowner Jessica Wallace, who still lives in her Mascot Flats apartment.

You could stand on the bottom floor, and the garbage was at least three feet deep, and squatters had been building fires at night on top of the garbage to keep themselves warm. It was such a horrible mess that in a weak moment I said, "You know, we need to come back here and help you finish this mess." And before I knew it, I was committed. —Jimmy Carter

At the time, Jessica was a single mother, sharing a room with her ten-year-old daughter in her mother's small apartment on Delancey Street. Her part-time job in the kitchen of an Alphabet City elementary school didn't pay very much, and so she couldn't

The Mascot Flats building was in terrible shape when President Carter arrived in 1984.

*Jessica Wallace in her nearly finished
Mascot Flats apartment*

afford an apartment of her own. "But one day," Jessica explains, "I passed by this building because the school where I worked was on the next block. A friend of mine was working on the building at the time, and I asked him what was going on. He told me that an organization called Habitat for Humanity was renovating the building for people with low incomes who needed a place to live. So I said, 'Well, that's me!' and he told me how to apply. The next day, when I finished work, I came here and put in the application, and I've pretty much been here ever since."

Jessica had no construction skills and could barely hammer a nail into a wall without hitting her finger, but she threw herself into the work regardless. "Sometimes the neighborhood people would try to discourage me," she recalls. "They'd say, 'You're not going to get that apartment. They're just going to let you do the work, but you're not going to actually get to live there.' That kind of talk was discouraging, but I kept on coming anyway because I needed a place to live and that motivated me. After work and also on Saturdays, I'd come here and work on the building. I came here in the cold and shoveled dirt and did whatever was asked of me. The requirement was once a week, but I wanted to work as much as I could so that I could get the apartment faster." As Jessica worked, she learned carpentry, masonry, tiling, and all the other basics of building construction.

"The best thing that's ever happened to me in life was when the Carters came here," Jessica declares. "The first time they came, my face lit up. They just wanted to work. From sunup to sundown, that's all they wanted to do."

I really got to know the Carters when they invited me to come to Chicago for the 1986 work project. We all slept on the floor in a hotel—even the Carters slept on the floor—but that didn't matter because we got up and worked just like we did here, from sunup to sundown. It's hard to fathom that anyone—not just the president, but anyone—would do what he's done for this organization. He really changed my life. —Jessica Wallace

"I remember, that first trip, I didn't particularly want to go," Rosalynn Carter admits. "I told Jimmy I would do anything but hammer, because I hadn't done that kind of work before, except maybe to hang a picture on the wall. I thought I would be sweeping up or helping with the food. But on the very first day, I was up on the second floor with two other volunteers, pulling up some linoleum.

What's It For? *Trowels are used to spread mortar between layers of brick. Most Habitat affiliates in the U.S. build houses out of wood, but affiliates in other countries often build homes out of brick.*

Well, we got it all clean, and it looked nice, and here comes a young man with a sheet of plywood, and

President Carter joins residents in celebrating the completion of the Mascot Flats project.

he says, 'The president said to nail this down.' We didn't know how many nails to put in it, but we got it nailed down, and since then I've been a carpenter."

The week that President and Mrs. Carter spent at the Mascot Flats proved to be so satisfying and so successful that every year since then the Carters have led a similar weeklong work project, building homes both in the United States and internationally. The impact of these projects is hard to measure, but no one doubts their importance to the growth of Habitat.

"The press just couldn't believe it," Rob DeRocker says. "Now you have sitting presidents who are willing to do Habitat work, but at that time the idea that a former leader of the free world would do anything more than a ceremonial hammer swing was just out of the question. So reporters would call me, and they'd say, 'No way, man. He's just going to be there for a photo, right?' And I'd say, 'No, he's going to be there all week.' And they'd say,

'The volunteers are going to stay at the church, but he'll be at a hotel, right?' And I'd say, 'No, he's going to be at the church, too.' They just couldn't believe what President Carter was doing, and overnight it put Habitat on the map. The publicity was the real benefit. All three national television networks did broadcasts, the *New York Times* ran stories, and *People* magazine ran a four-page spread. It was the hammer swing heard 'round the world."

FROM THAT POINT ON, Habitat's growth surged. People began to hear about the organization; and once they did, many started to participate. By the time the Carters completed their twenty-fifth work project in May 2008, Habitat had expanded to include more than two thousand affiliates and more than one million volunteers. In November 2008, the organization began work on its three-hundred-thousandth house—completed by the Collier County, Florida, affiliate in April 2009.

Certainly, none of this would have been possible without the contributions of Millard Fuller, Clarence Jordan, and Jimmy Carter. Jordan, for his part, provided the ideas that formed the basis of Habitat's ideology, especially the idea that faith means little without action. Fuller contributed the drive and salesmanship necessary to take Jordan's ideas and create an organization that would spread them beyond the boundaries of Koinonia Farm. Even so, it wasn't until President Carter added his prestige and his own considerable powers of persuasion that Fuller's cause became the international success it is today.

Detroit, Michigan

Clarksdale, Mississi

Huntsville, Texas

San Antonio, Texas

Anniston, Alaba

Beattyville, Kentucky

Berea, Kentu

2. Shelter

A FEW MONTHS BEFORE Allen Kinder's second birthday, he and his parents moved into a small rental home on Red Oak Street in Charleston, West Virginia. The single-family house was in bad shape, and the neighborhood wasn't any better, but it was all the Kinders could afford. A year later, Allen's parents separated, and his mother, Debbie Kinder, was left to pay all of the bills on her own. "We were probably about as low as you can get," Allen remembers.

Among the many problems with the house was the roof. One night during a rainstorm, Allen woke up and called out for his mother because something was falling on his head. "I went into his room," Debbie Kinder says, "and, sure enough, a big leak had busted through the ceiling and was pouring water down on his bed."

The landlord fixed that leak but not the many others. According to Allen, "We'd get terrible leaks that left really bad stains in the ceiling. I remember

Allen Kinder in the living room of the house on Red Oak Street

EXAMPLES OF SUBSTANDARD HOUSING IN DIFFERENT COMMUNITIES AROUND THE UNITED STATES

The Kinders' house on Red Oak Street had siding made out of asbestos, which has since been banned because it causes cancer.

one leak that made a big stain right where you walked into the house. I'd always try to distract kids who came over. I'd say, 'Race you to my room' just to get them past the stains, because I thought they were so embarrassing."

A much more dangerous problem was the house's careless electrical wiring. The circuits hadn't been installed properly, and the mice that roamed the house chewed off much of the insulation that covered the wires. As a result, Allen and his mother often got electric shocks when they turned on a light. The worst switch was in the bathroom. "Whenever we turned on that light, we'd get shocked," Allen confirms. "So we started wearing rubber gloves, but the problem got worse, and we didn't have enough money to hire an electrician. One day, my mom got shocked so badly that she was knocked unconscious. I was about eight years old at the time, and I remember walking in to find her unconscious on the floor. That was pretty scary. I was old enough to know that something was wrong but not old enough to know what to do about it."

Debbie Kinder had been cleaning the bathroom when her wet rag accidentally grazed the light switch. The water in the rag acted as a conductor, and she received a large jolt of electricity. "It felt as though a lightning bolt had hit me," she says, "and I lost consciousness. I wasn't out very long, but Allen was scared to death.

Debbie Kinder in her bedroom on Red Oak Street. Because the house had no doors, even on the bathroom, she and Allen used curtains for privacy.

We asked the landlord to fix the problem, but for the longest time she wouldn't." Finally, when the bathtub and toilet began falling through the rotted-out bathroom floor, the landlord sent a repairman, who fixed the floor and the wiring in the bathroom but not anything else in the house. Shortly after the Kinders moved out, the property on Red Oak Street burned to the ground. The cause was an electrical fire. "We got out of there just in time," Allen says with a sigh.

Even though the house on Red Oak Street was in terrible shape, the rent that Debbie Kinder paid was high because there was a housing shortage in Charleston and the landlords knew it. Debbie had looked all over town, and there simply weren't any decent places available at a reasonable cost.

> Our children are our future, and we have to take care of them. I'm not talking about giving them the best toys or the most expensive clothes. I'm talking about basic needs like a safe house in a neighborhood without drugs or crime, a healthy house without mold or leaks or mice or anything else that might make you sick. —Debbie Kinder

"We went without a lot of things," Allen remembers. "My mom always made sure that I was fed, but I know that she went without meals sometimes. She was working two jobs, and then she started college so that she could get a better job and afford a new house. But going to school put even more pressure on her."

Although Debbie Kinder was already having trouble managing her situation, she began taking college courses because she was determined to make a better life for herself and her son. Her ambition was to become a social worker so that she could help families in need, like her own.

"The problem with our housing system," Debbie explains, "is that sometimes you have people living in houses that aren't safe and aren't big enough to hold the entire family. On top of that, you have all the stress of making ends meet, of buying enough groceries just to feed everybody. I mean, there's nothing worse than having your kid come to you and say, 'I'm hungry. Can I please have that hot dog?' And you have to say, 'No, we have to save that hot dog for dinner.' Those kinds of things can put so much stress on a family that parents can become abusive. It's not because they want to hurt their kids; it's because they don't know how to cope with their situation."

Debbie first heard about Habitat for Humanity from a public service announcement that she saw on television. After seeing the commercial a few more times, she called up the local Charleston affiliate, Habitat for Humanity of Kanawha and Putnam County, to ask for an application. Unfortunately, a volunteer at the affiliate told her, mistakenly, that divorced single mothers didn't qualify for Habitat homes. "So I didn't finish the application," Debbie says. But when she began attending college a year later, the subject of Habitat soon came up again.

It turned out that one of her social work professors sat on the affiliate's board of directors and sometimes mentioned Habitat in class. After one of those classes, Debbie spoke with the professor privately and explained her situation. "The professor told me that being divorced wouldn't matter, and she encouraged me to apply because she knew I was a hard worker. I did, and I was so thankful that God put her in my path, because if she hadn't been there, I would never have known I was eligible.

"I knew I wanted something better for my son," Debbie emphasizes, "and I knew I wasn't ever going to be able to get a regular homeowner's loan—at least not until I graduated from college, and that was too far away. The dangers in that house were too present and too strong for me not to do something right away."

THE FOUNDERS OF HABITAT FOR HUMANITY of Kanawha and Putnam County, to which Debbie applied for a house in 1998, were Bill and Peggy Londeree. "I first met Millard Fuller at a faith-at-work conference in Ohio in late 1969," Bill recalls, "and because of what Millard had to say about Koinonia, my wife and I went down there to live for about four years during the early 1970s." Not long after the Fullers left for Zaire, the Londerees returned to their home state of West Virginia. But the Londerees kept in touch with the Fullers, and not long after Millard and Linda returned from Zaire in 1976, Bill and Peggy went down to Americus to visit them.

"Originally," Bill continues, "Millard thought that Habitat was going to be primarily an international ministry. He had a little house in Americus that he called the 'international headquarters,' which Peggy and I thought was pretty funny when we visited. We always knew Millard liked to dream big. But not long after we got back from that visit, we began noticing a few Habitat chapters getting started around the country. We kind of thought, jiminy Christmas, something should be done here in West Virginia. I mean, if anyplace needs housing, it's surely West Virginia. So we got to thinking about starting our own affiliate.

"At first, we mostly approached people we knew, either in our church or in the community," Bill continues. "We just asked people we thought might be interested whether they would come to an organizational meeting." At this time, in mid-1986, there weren't many Habitat affiliates in the United States and none at all in West Virginia. Few people in Charleston, according to Bill, had even heard of Habitat, and that made the organizing go rather slowly. So did Bill's need to work full-time to support his family. As a result, almost a year and a half passed before he and Peggy held the first organizational meeting in their suburban Charleston living room. At that meeting in January 1988, the decision was made to move ahead.

If a child can't feel confident about who he is when he's little, how confident can he be when he's older? If he grows up with a poor standard of living and nothing to be proud of, how is he going to learn to be a proud and productive adult? He's going to think, Why try? I'm always going to have this life. —Debbie Kinder

Today, in order to become a Habitat affiliate, a group of interested people has to commit to an extensive process that typically takes eighteen months to complete. The process is long and thorough because Habitat's leadership wants to be sure that all new affiliates thoroughly understand Habitat methods and philosophy. In 1988, however, the affiliation process was simpler, and the Charleston group was able to gain approval in just two months, at which point Bill Londeree became its first executive director.

"Of course, when you start something new, nobody knows what it is," Bill explains. "There's a lot of groundwork that you have to do just to get the name out, and I must have spoken at every church in Kanawha and Putnam counties. I met with anybody who would have me, and it just kind of grew over the years.

"Early on," he remembers, "we went to the city leaders of Charleston and showed them some of our ideas and asked them to donate some land to us. They thought we were absolutely crazy because they didn't have much faith in volunteer organizations back then. But we convinced them to donate a piece of land in one of the worst parts of Charleston, and we built a house there. After that, when the city saw that what we were doing worked, they really got behind us and started donating more land. Success breeds success, you know?"

When Debbie Kinder applied for a Habitat house, she knew that getting one wasn't going to be easy. To begin with, most Habitat applicants get turned down.

"We approve families four times a year," explains Tina Rhodes, the family services director at Habitat for Humanity of Kanawha and Putnam County. "We begin by estimating how many houses

we're going to build during the next year and a half. For us, that's about fifteen houses, because we build about ten a year. So we need to have fifteen families on our list at any given time." As houses get built, new families leave the list and others are added.

The cut-off dates are April 1, July 1, October 1, and January 1. Once the application period closes, the family selection committee begins its work. This is the group within the affiliate that decides which applicants will become partner families. During the next three months, the members of the family selection committee will review all the applications and visit each family twice in its current home.

All Habitat affiliates use three main criteria in determining which families should be approved. These criteria are need, ability to pay, and willingness to partner. In considering need, the family selection committee looks at each family's current living situation and asks itself a number of questions: Is the family's current house falling apart? Is it overcrowded? Is it located in a dangerous neighborhood?

The family's ability to pay is also important, because Habitat is not a giveaway program. Affiliates don't make any profit on the houses they build or the home loans they make. This is why Habitat houses are affordable, even to people with low incomes. But the partner families do have to pay full price for the houses. "Whatever the mortgage is going to be," Tina Rhodes explains, "they have to show that they have enough income and that they have halfway decent credit."

NAPLES IS A RELATIVELY PROSPEROUS CITY in southern Florida. Even so, not far from Naples, there are fathers and mothers trapped in low-paying jobs who live with their children in substandard houses like this run-down shack.

Finally, the family selection committee considers each family's willingness to partner — that is, how prepared the family is to do its share of the work. On a Habitat project, that means attending classes on home ownership and working hundreds of hours on construction sites.

About a month before the family selection committee meets to take its vote, Tina Rhodes lets the members know how many slots are available. Typically, there are only two or three open slots for eighteen to twenty applicants.

The families who don't receive houses are sent letters telling them why they were turned down. Sometimes the reason is that the family's need isn't great enough. Maybe its current house is unpleasant but still livable. Sometimes the reason has to do with the family's ability to pay. The parents may have a bad credit rating because they once borrowed money that they didn't pay back, or perhaps their income is just too low to afford even a Habitat mortgage. Sometimes the reason is that the family selection committee had concerns about the applicant's willingness to partner. Sometimes, of course, the reason is simply that there aren't enough houses to go around.

Fortunately for Debbie Kinder, she didn't receive one of those letters. Instead, she was approved for a house.

WHEN A FAMILY BUYS A HOUSE on the commercial real estate market, it typically makes a down payment and borrows the rest of the purchase price from a mortgage lender. If a family makes a down payment of 10 percent, then it owns 10 percent of the house and the mortgage lender owns the remaining 90 percent. As the loan is paid off, the family's percentage of ownership goes up and the lender's goes down. The portion of the house that the family owns is called its equity in the house.

Habitat affiliates require only a small down payment because few low-income families can afford more than that. Instead, partner families are required to contribute sweat equity. The phrase *sweat equity* refers to an ownership interest created by the sweat of a person's labor. "I think that makes so much difference," Rosalynn Carter says.

Habitat for Humanity of Kanawha and Putnam County requires all two-parent partner families to contribute 500 hours of work toward the construction of their home as well as the homes of other partner families. Single parents, such as Debbie Kinder, have to put in 250 hours. The sweat equity requirement works out to two full days per adult per month from the time a family is approved until its house is built.

What's It For?
On Habitat job sites, hammers are used most often to drive nails. However, if a ladder won't stand straight, you can level it by using the claw of a hammer to dig out the ground under one foot.

In addition, all partner families are required to attend fifteen home ownership classes on subjects ranging from creating a spending plan and learning how to save to getting along with neighbors and basic home repair. The time that they spend in these classes counts toward their sweat equity requirement, half of which must be completed before construction on that family's house can begin.

"For me," Debbie Kinder recalls, "getting in my sweat equity was really hard. I was working, I was taking night classes, and I also had Allen to care for, so it was very difficult for me to find the

Allen and Debbie Kinder at the dedication ceremony for their new Habitat home

time. In the end, I had to drop one of my college classes so that I could make sure I got to those homeowner's classes."

According to Tina Rhodes, "The thing that I remember most about Debbie is that she was really scared for Allen's safety. I think there were drugs in her neighborhood and other problems that made her really fearful, which may have been why she was so committed."

Because Debbie was raising Allen on her own, she often had to bring him to her nighttime Habitat classes. As Tina Rhodes recalls, Allen at age eight was "a wonderful child with a sweet attitude. He came with his mother to a lot of activities that children don't usually attend because Debbie had trouble finding child care. He would sit in the lobby and do his homework, always quiet and always very respectful. I remember really well the day his house was dedicated. Nationwide Insurance had sponsored the construction, and so we held the dedication at the local Nationwide office. Allen was there, and he was just glowing. He stood up in front with his mom, and he had a big old smile on his face. You didn't hear a whole lot out of that boy, because he was so quiet, but he had a lot of joy in him that day, and it showed."

Allen still has a lot of joy when he thinks about his Habitat house. "When we first moved in, my mother and I had this devotional thing we'd do. Every night, we would name all the people we were thankful for, especially the people at Habitat."

In fact, Debbie Kinder was so thankful that she agreed to join the affiliate's board of directors, bringing with her a perspective that had been lacking: the perspective of a low-income person. "At the time," Tina Rhodes says, "everyone on our board was pretty high income, so they didn't have that perspective. They hadn't lived that kind of life and faced those challenges. But Debbie brought with her that point of view and also a new focus on the partner families."

Although someone else might have been intimidated, Debbie wasn't afraid to speak up, because she knew that what she was saying was right. "I've dealt with so many different things in my life that there isn't much I haven't seen or experienced," she explains. "Because of that, I can go in front of a group of potential Habitat homeowners and say, 'Yes, you can make ends meet. Yes, you can own a house. Yes, you can go to college and be successful. I know you can, because I've done it.'

"I was no spring chicken when I went to college," she continues. "I waited until my late twenties because I thought I wasn't smart enough. I'd been told that my whole life—'You're not smart enough. You'll never make it to college'—and for a while, I believed it. But I don't believe it anymore because I know it isn't true. Instead, I believe that no matter what you've been through,

The Habitat house in North Charleston where the Kinders live today

you can make your situation better if you put your mind to it. If you love your kids, and you want them to be productive members of society, you have to think that way. Red Oak Street wasn't what

I wanted for my son. I wanted him to be able to play and make friends and not be embarrassed when they came over because they'd see a mouse running across the floor or get shocked turning on the bathroom light. I didn't want those things for him.

"Of course," she admits, "it really helps if you have a support system that also believes in you. Habitat provided that support system for me. The people there were so encouraging. They knew how much I was doing, what I was struggling with, and how rough it was—and they were always there with something good to say."

LIKE ALLEN KINDER, Amber Ferrell also lived in a run-down house. Hers was located on a plot of land next door to her grandparents' house, about a mile outside the Charleston city limits. She was in first grade when her family moved into that house.

According to Amber, "I never knew what was going to happen. There was always something going wrong with that house— something falling apart, something not working right. The holes in the walls made it really cold in the wintertime. I remember one hole above the bathtub that was so big you could almost see outside, and the back of the house was in such bad shape that it had to be held up with jacks. My sister and I used to joke that some guy named Jack was holding our house up."

The Ferrells' home was small, with only two bedrooms. Amber's parents slept in one, and she and her older sister, Pam, shared the other. Her younger brother, Jeremy, slept in a nearby

ACCORDING TO THE UNITED NATIONS, more than 1.1 billion people worldwide live in inadequate housing in urban slums such as this one in Phnom Penh, Cambodia.

alcove. "It was right off our room," Amber remembers, "and there wasn't any door or windows, so I guess it was more like a walk-in closet that had been turned into a room.

"At the time," she continues, "the house seemed normal to us. But when we talk about it now, we realize how difficult it was to live there. Kids can sense when their parents aren't happy about something, and my parents were always mad. Something was always going wrong with the house, and they'd have to patch it back together with whatever means they had."

Amber was so embarrassed by the poor condition of her house that it kept her from making friends. "The house was a daily reminder of how little we actually had," she explains. "When the place where you put everything you have, where you spend your life, is in such bad condition, then of course it's going to cause you to have self-esteem issues. I think that as kids we all tried to act as though nothing was wrong. Other kids would talk about their houses, and I'd say, 'Yeah, yeah, me, too.' But when it came time to sleep over or something, I'd have to say, 'Oh, no, let's not do it at my house.' I didn't want anybody seeing that house. Even though in some ways I thought it was normal, I knew deep down that it wasn't something to show off or be proud of. What I really thought was *Why would someone want to be friends with a person who doesn't have anything?*"

When her grandparents were away, Amber would often ask her mother for the key to their house so that she could go over there and "chill out for a while." She was comfortable there, she says, because

> I wasn't so much afraid of monsters as I was of actual people, because the house always made noises at night. When the wind blew, it just made lots of scary noises, and I could never really tell whether it was just the wind or someone outside. —Amber Ferrell

her grandparents' house was much nicer than her own. Later, when Habitat for Humanity of Kanawha and Putnam County approved the Ferrells for a new home, the decision was made to tear down the old house and build a new one on the same land, which Amber's grandparents donated to Habitat. "When Habitat knocked that house down, it was a great day," Amber laughs.

It took about nine months to build the Ferrells' new house. During much of that time, Amber's family lived next door with her grandparents. According to Tina Rhodes, it was a familiar sight to see the faces of Amber, Pam, and Jeremy pressed up against the glass of their grandparents' windows, watching closely as their new house took shape.

The Ferrells finally moved in just as Amber was finishing eighth grade. "There was definitely a change," she recalls. "I had a new sense of pride, I guess, to tell people about the house, invite them over, and not be ashamed of friends seeing where I lived."

Tina Rhodes witnessed the same change, although from a different perspec-

Amber Ferrell (left) with her parents and brother, Jeremy, at the dedication of their Habitat house

tive. "The Ferrells are pretty typical of the families we work with. I see people all the time who've been beaten down by life, who might not have the best education, and who are pretty shy as a result. But as they go through the Habitat program, their confidence builds, and you can see a real change in their attitude. It's something I've seen over and over again with families. It's as though they become new people."

Valdosta, Georgia

Asikuma, Gha

New Orleans, Louisiana

Alambaraikuppam, Inc

Detroit, Michigan

Blantyre, Mala

3. How to Design a House

HABITAT FOR HUMANITY'S MISSION is to build simple, decent homes, but the words *simple* and *decent* can describe many different types of homes. The final form that each Habitat house takes depends on where the house is built and who does the building. A Habitat house in New York City, for example, won't look like one in Charleston, West Virginia, and a Habitat house in India won't look like one in Romania.

An important issue is how many houses are going to be built. Some U.S. affiliates build just one or two houses a year. For them, the design process is often informal. Typically, a small affiliate will rely on a relationship with an experienced local builder. That builder may begin with a house design that he or she has used before on a different project, spending only a day or two adapting it to meet Habitat's construction guidelines. But affiliates that build on a large scale, constructing neighborhoods of thirty or forty homes at a time, will put their projects through a much more extensive design process.

HOMES THAT HABITAT VOLUNTEERS
HAVE BUILT AROUND THE WORLD

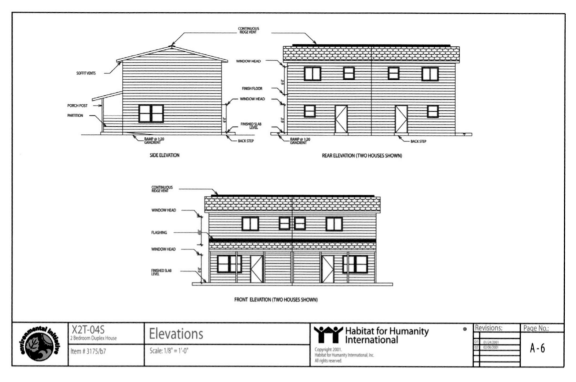

CONTINUOUS RIDGE VENT

SOFFIT VENTS

WINDOW HEAD

PORCH POST

PARTITION

FINISH FLOOR

WINDOW HEAD

FINISHED SLAB LEVEL

BACK STEP

RAMP @ 1:20 GRADIENT

SIDE ELEVATION

RAMP @ 1:20 GRADIENT

BACK STEP

REAR ELEVATION (TWO HOUSES SHOWN)

CONTINUOUS RIDGE VENT

WINDOW HEAD

FLASHING

WINDOW HEAD

FINISHED SLAB LEVEL

FRONT ELEVATION (TWO HOUSES SHOWN)

| X2T-04S
2 Bedroom Duplex House
Item # 3175/b7 | Elevations

Scale: 1/8" = 1'-0" | Habitat for Humanity International

Copyright 2001.
Habitat for Humanity International, Inc.
All rights reserved. | Revisions:
01 01/24/2001
02 02/06/2001 | Page No.:

A-6 |

A floor plan (right) and elevations for a two-family Habitat home

BACK STEP/ RAMP

COMMON WALL

F

KITCHEN/ DINING
16'-0" x 11'-5"

20'-0"

24'-0"

Habitat for Humanity International

LIVING
16'-0" x 11'-8"

UP

RAMP @ 1:20 GRADIENT

PARTITION WALL

PORCH

PORCH POST

FIRST FLOOR

Before any construction can begin, a set of plans needs to be drawn up. These plans must include a floor layout, showing the size and arrangement of the rooms; a set of views called elevations, showing what the house will look like on the outside; and other drawings that show how the roof will be constructed, how the kitchen cabinets will be installed, and so on.

U.S. affiliates, in particular, build in many different architectural styles to suit local tastes. As a resource, Habitat for Humanity International (the name of the parent organization) maintains a large database of house plans—some that its own architects have created, others that affiliates have developed and contributed. In a few cases, these plans can be used as they are, but they usually undergo some modification. Different regions of the country, for example, have different heating and cooling requirements depending on their climates. A house in northern Maine needs more insulation and a much larger heating system than a house in southern Florida. The house in Florida, on the other hand, needs air-conditioning in every room, while the house in Maine doesn't need any. Beyond these differences, affiliates need to observe local governmental building codes, and most also like to include partner families in the design process.

"Usually, affiliates will work with volunteer architects to adapt existing designs and draw up permit-ready sets of plans," Steve Weir explains. An architect himself, Steve helped found the Habitat affiliate in Oakland, California, before becoming Habitat's head of global program development. "In order to do a good job, the architect really needs to involve the homeowners and, when the project is an entire neighborhood, the community as well. Especially in the case of building a neighborhood of twenty or thirty homes, I would expect the architect or designer to help the community decide how the homes should be organized and what the final floor plans and construction details should be. For instance, most mothers spend a lot of time in their kitchens, so where should the kitchen go? Should it go in the back of the house, because that way mothers can watch their kids playing in the backyard? Or should it go in the front of the house, because most of the kids will be playing on the street?"

I was looking for a better way to integrate my faith with my day-to-day job when I saw a news report about the very first Carter build in New York City. There was an 800 number to call, and I called the number, and the person who answered said, "Oh, we're just starting an affiliate in your area." And so I joined its board of directors. —Steve Weir

Once these basic choices have been made, there are still some details that each partner family gets to decide for itself. For example, one family may like carpeting, while another prefers wood flooring. "In the U.S.," Steve continues, "even after an affiliate settles on a basic house design, a partner family can still decide it wants to add a fence or a washer/dryer. Homeowners always have options, but we don't create a brand-new house plan for each individual homeowner."

The primary challenge that architects face when designing Habitat homes in the United States is fitting the home into an existing community or neighborhood while still keeping it affordable for a low-income family. Think for a moment of the large public housing projects that city governments began to build in the 1950s. These unpleasant, isolated, and often danger-

ALTHOUGH MOST HABITAT HOMES in the United States are built using standardized designs, there is still plenty of local variation. This Habitat home in Taos, New Mexico, for example, uses bricks made of adobe — a traditional southwestern building material made of sand, water, and clay that keeps homes cool during the hot desert summers.

ous apartment blocks may have been built with noble intentions, but what they ended up doing was separating the poor from the rest of the community.

Habitat's goal is to integrate people rather than separate them. It does this, in part, by designing homes that are inexpensive to build yet are still handsome enough to fit in with the rest of the homes in a stable neighborhood. When a Habitat home looks out of place, that's usually because it's the *nicest*-looking house in a neighborhood that has deteriorated. In that case, a Habitat home often becomes a focal point for the neighborhood's revitalization. "We often build

homes in areas that are really run down, with no care given to the community," President Carter says. "But when we come back six or seven years later, we usually find that the entire neighborhood has been rebuilt and renewed—not by rich people moving in, but by the original residents repairing and improving their homes."

As an organization, Habitat for Humanity has committed itself to serving people who can't otherwise find affordable housing. In the United States, where the government provides housing for the very poor and banks give housing loans to people with at least moderate incomes, Habitat serves an economic class often known as the working poor. These are people with regular jobs who make too much money to qualify for government aid and too little money to qualify for a bank loan.

In developing countries such as Kenya and Cambodia, however, the situation is altogether different. There is no government housing for the poor, and the banks don't offer much in the way of housing loans. In these countries, Habitat serves nearly everyone.

"If you look at developing countries," Steve Weir explains, "as little as 10 percent of the population has access to formal financing. So if you go to the Kibera slum in Kenya—the largest slum in Africa, where over a million people live—you'll find people living there who are government workers, teachers, nurses. In the United States, these people would be considered middle class. But in Kenya, they live in a slum because they have no access to home financing."

An Indonesian partner family stands in front of its nearly complete Habitat home. Mukhtar (left) holds two-year-old Nurwahdiah, while Usmiah (right) holds five-month-old Badrudin. Their house is part of a Habitat development called Pasi Aron. When completed, Pasi Aron will provide housing for six thousand families who lost their homes in the 2004 Indian Ocean tsunami.

The design process for building Habitat homes outside the United States is similar in one way to the process within the United States: its focus on local circumstances. But otherwise, there is a world of difference. In the United States, the most important design considerations relate to local building codes and the aesthetics of the house—that is, the way the house looks, especially the architectural style in which it's built. Overseas, however, especially in developing countries in Africa and Asia, considerations relating to the basic health of the partner families and the culture in which they live are much more pressing.

The purpose of building codes is to ensure that all new construction is safe. In the developing world, however, few governments have or enforce building codes, so Habitat has devised its own set of standards to promote the health and well-being of Habitat homeowners. These standards include a requirement that for each member of a partner family, the home has at least 37.5 square feet of space. That is, a house built for a family of six needs to have at least 225 square feet of floor space. (In comparison, the average size of a Habitat house within the United States is 1,100 square feet.) Another basic requirement is that every Habitat home have access to safe drinking water.

Habitat's international affiliates also pay close attention to the culture of the countries in which they build. On some Pacific islands, for example, the custom is that no one can be higher than the tribal chief. For this reason, the houses of the chiefs have two doors. The chief enters through a normal door, while visitors to his house enter through an intentionally low second door that requires

IN PAPUA NEW GUINEA, where houses are often built on stilts, Habitat follows the local tradition. According to Steve Weir, the practice began when Christian missionaries saw that livestock (mostly pigs) were wandering freely into and out of homes and warned the local people of the health hazard that posed.

them to stoop. A Habitat home built for such a chief would have to be designed to include two doors. Otherwise, the chief wouldn't want to live in it.

"I'll share a related story with you," Steve Weir laughs. "We had an agreement to work with another organization that was very experienced at water and sanitation. Habitat was going to build the houses, and this other agency was going to build the toilets—which were going to be detached from the homes, like outhouses. So they built these tiny little boxes behind each house. But the building site was a beach where a community of fishermen lived. For generations, these people had used the ocean as their toilet, and it had been a wonderful experience, feeling the cool sea breeze and the water around your legs. Now they were being asked to use a small, cramped, dark, smelly box. Well, you can imagine how they voted. About six months later, this other agency came back to see how their toilets were working, and almost all of them had been turned into chicken coops."

A PARTICULARLY INTERESTING EXAMPLE of the ways in which international affiliates adapt building plans to suit local conditions involves the small Brazilian village of Varjada. Located in the countryside of northeastern Brazil, where the terrain is hilly and the climate is very dry, Varjada is a poor community of about 175 families. Some of its residents are the descendants of Portuguese colonists; others have native Indian ancestry. For generations, the village has been known for the fine embroidery skills of its women and also for its poverty.

Nearly everyone who lives in Varjada walks from place to place because no one can afford a car. When national affiliate Habitat Brasil began working in Varjada in 2005, this lack of transportation posed a serious problem because the nearest source of water was two miles away. During Varjada's long dry season, which lasts from September until May, the women of the village, including the older girls, had to spend four hours a day walking up and down a steep hill to fetch water for drinking, cooking, bathing, and cleaning.

Another serious problem in Varjada related to the way that the homes were constructed. Before Habitat Brasil began building there, all the homes in Varjada were made of *taipa,* a traditional mixture of mud and clay similar to adobe. *Taipa* is easy to come by, of course, but it's not a good construction material because it doesn't weather well and requires regular patching, especially when it's used on rooftops. In fact, *taipa* roofs leak badly. "At night, we

The dry, hilly landscape that surrounds the village of Varjada, Brazil

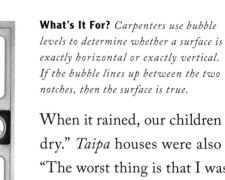

couldn't sleep," recalls Maria Josefa de Oliveira, who raised her eight children in a *taipa* house. "We were uncomfortable and nervous. When it rained, our children slept under the kitchen table to stay dry." *Taipa* houses were also notoriously difficult to keep clean. "The worst thing is that I was ashamed and embarrassed," Maria's daughter-in-law, Valdenice de Oliveira, says. "I cleaned and cleaned and was never able to get it the way I wanted."

Even worse, the *taipa* in the walls caused grave health problems among the children of the village. The mud and clay provided an ideal breeding ground for a species of blood-sucking insect known as the kissing bug. (The children of Varjada, who speak Portuguese, call it *barbeiro,* meaning "the barber.") The bite of the kissing bug spreads a potentially fatal illness called Chagas's disease, which eats away at a person's internal organs.

Varjada resident Marcone Ramos Herculano stands in front of his old taipa *house.*

*Marcone Ramos Herculano and Antonia Maria do Paraiso on the porch
of the new Habitat house in which they live with their two children*

In 2004, Habitat Brasil formed a partnership with the Methodist
Church to develop a project for Varjada, which has a strong
Methodist congregation. The original plan was to build new
bathrooms for fifty of the existing *taipa* houses. "But when we got
there," remembers project director Claudio Braga, "the people asked
us, 'Can we live in the bathrooms?' and we realized immediately
that it made no sense to build new bathrooms when the houses were
in such bad condition."

The Varjada plan was soon revised. Instead of building bathrooms, Habitat Brasil decided to build completely new houses,
which were designed specifically to address the village's health and
water problems. To begin with, the new homes were built not with

Each of the new Varjada cisterns holds 16,000 liters of water, or about 4,250 gallons. Most residents use buckets to bring the water into the house as they need it.

taipa but with concrete and brick. Once the mud was gone, the kissing bugs also disappeared, and so did the Chagas's disease.

The Habitat architects also solved the water problem with a clever roof design. Their idea was to channel the rainwater, which normally ran off the roof onto the ground, into pipes that drained into a large cistern, or collection tank, built alongside each house. During the three-month rainy season, runoff from the roof would fill the cistern, providing enough water to meet the needs of the homeowners during the dry season.

"Before we went to Varjada, we had arranged for Caixa, the national bank of Brazil, to provide financing for the fifty bathrooms in our original plan," Claudio recalls. "Afterward, we went back to the bank and explained the situation and came away with enough financing for fifty new homes—each with two bedrooms, a small living room, a kitchen, *and* a new bathroom." Additional financing has since enabled Habitat Brasil to build 80 more homes in Varjada for a total of 130. The affiliate has also arranged for the construction of a small medical clinic, and plans are under way for a new school.

Poor people often have a lot of promises made to them from different sources—from governments, from charities, and so forth. Often, these promises are broken. Habitat for Humanity doesn't break promises, and that creates hope. —Jimmy Carter

Now that the construction of the cisterns has freed the women of Varjada from the drudgery of fetching water, they are able to spend more time on other things. The girls can go to school, and the older women can pursue their embroidery. According to Claudio, "Before, they could only sew at night. This led to many vision problems, because sewing at night is very bad for the eyes. But now they have time to sew during the day, in the sunlight, and they can be much more productive."

With the help of both Habitat Brasil and another charitable organization called World Vision International, the women of Varjada have banded together to market their work collectively. As a result, their incomes have become much less precarious. Instead of living on $1.50 a day, they now earn about $7.50 per day. "In the beginning, we didn't have faith in the project," says Severina Guilermina Ferreira, the leader of the women's embroidery cooperative. "But we had faith in God, and we saw the Habitat people coming here and working, and we began to see these were people we could have faith in."

Udon Thani, Thailand

New Iberia, Louisia

Fosu, Ghana

Alambaraikuppam, In

Guayaquil, Ecuador

Piesang River, South A

4. Service

A s President Carter says, all people have the duty to help others who are in need. The problem is the chasm that separates affluent people, or even everyday people, from those who have little or nothing. Danielle Weir, the daughter of Habitat's Steve Weir, experienced this chasm for the first time when she was just four years old, and the memory has stayed with her ever since.

"One of my earliest memories is of baking chocolate-chip cookies for a homeless man who lived around the corner from my home in Berkeley, California," Danielle says. "He slept in the doorway of a store at night, and I remember wanting to make him cookies because he was a grandfatherly man and I had this internal picture of him becoming my buddy. So my mother helped me bake the cookies, and we walked down the street to where he was, and when we got there, I became afraid all of a sudden. The reality of talking to this man, whom I'd never communicated with, seemed scary. I remember my mom saying over and over again, 'My daughter

VOLUNTEERS OF DIFFERENT NATIONALITIES WORKING
ON HABITAT HOMES AROUND THE WORLD

made these cookies for you. My daughter made these cookies for you. We want you to have them.' He never responded, so we just put the plate down in front of him and walked back home.

"I remember being a little shocked and disappointed," Danielle goes on. "But since then I've thought about how lonely he must have been—people walking right by him every day without acknowledging him. I can only imagine how difficult it must have been for him and how, after being overlooked every day, he might have simply stopped acknowledging others, too."

The Weir family in Sri Lanka, with Danielle and her father in the foreground

Danielle's experience of poverty was actually just beginning. When she was eleven, she moved with her family to Sri Lanka, an island nation off the southern coast of India, to which her father had been posted by Habitat. In Sri Lanka, she was exposed to poverty much, much worse than anything she had seen in the United States.

"Before the move, my knowledge of poverty was limited to a vague understanding that some people are homeless," Danielle says. "But in Sri Lanka, we visited slums where the children ran around barefoot and not fully clothed, where the houses were just random pieces of wood and tin somehow fastened together. Inside these houses, there was nothing, except maybe bowls or something to eat out of and maybe a blanket to lie on."

Fifteen years later, Danielle works as a case manager for Summit House in Charlotte, North Carolina. Summit House is an alternative to prison for women convicted of nonviolent crimes who are pregnant or have young children. Danielle's job is to help these women stay out of jail, keep their families together, and reenter society as productive citizens. "Especially after Sri Lanka," Danielle says, "I became more aware and more passionate about advocating for those in need of assistance."

According to Danielle, she has learned two important lessons from her experiences as the child of a Habitat staff member. One is that all people, not just the rich, have the ability to serve those who live in more difficult circumstances. "I know this," Danielle explains, "because my family is very ordinary, very everyday. When we moved to Sri Lanka, there wasn't anything significant or special about us that made us stand out from our neighbors. My parents simply felt a faith calling to serve with Habitat, and so we did. Seeing that play out, I've realized that it doesn't have to take an extraordinary person to improve the lot of poor communities in the world. It takes everyday people who are willing to do it."

What's It For? *Interlocking blocks are used to build homes in Asia and Africa, where timber can be hard to find. Composed of soil and cement, these blocks, like LEGOs, have projections that align them automatically, so walls made from them are straight.*

The second lesson Danielle learned is the importance of serving not just some people but all people in need. "Sometimes, the easy way out is to be selective," she says, "to help only those people you can identify with, those you feel comfortable around. But I think you need to be willing to help anybody, especially people who are different from you. Building relationships through service restores dignity to those being served, creates a greater sense of unity, and ultimately promotes peace."

Jimmy Carter learned about service from his mother, Lillian— or Miss Lillian, as she was known all over Sumter County. A registered nurse, Miss Lillian taught her children by example. She treated all people with equal kindness, no matter their race or economic standing. "Mother reached out to the poorest and most persecuted people in our community and treated them on a completely equal basis," President Carter explains. "After my daddy began to earn enough money so that he didn't really need my mother's income, she began to do most of her nursing on a pro bono basis. The poor families that she nursed were supposed to pay her, but she knew, and I knew, and everybody knew, that they couldn't, and she didn't expect them to."

STUDENTS AT FOREST HILLS NORTHERN HIGH SCHOOL in Grand Rapids showed great initiative when they committed themselves to building a Habitat house in their Michigan community. Raising the seventy thousand dollars they needed through donations, dances, dinners, and the sale of decorated two-by-fours, the students also volunteered more than thirty-two hundred hours on the job site.

In 1966, when Miss Lillian was sixty-eight years old, she entered the Peace Corps, which sent her to India. For two years, she worked as a nurse in a medical clinic in Vikhroli, a poor factory town outside Mumbai (then called Bombay). On her seventieth birthday, she wrote a letter to her children from Vikhroli. "I didn't dream that in this remote corner of the world, so far away from the people and material things that I had always considered so necessary, I would discover what life is really all about, sharing yourself with others—and accepting their love for you is the most precious gift of all."

"My mother was the first person to give me a glimmer of the ethic of service," President Carter continues. "But Millard Fuller was the one who gave me the opportunity to put that aspect of my faith into action. Habitat made it easy, and I don't think there's any doubt that the work of Habitat is inspired by the same sense of giving and equality that my mother stood for in her life."

Jason Carter, the president's grandson, knows something about Habitat, having taken part in the 2002 Carter Work Project in Durban, South Africa. He also knows a good deal about Carter family history. According to Jason, "An important reason that Habitat means so much to my family is that it arose in the same place that my family did, and it's defined by the same small-town, Sumter County ethic. It's the ethic that inspired Clarence Jordan to start Koinonia Farm

> My grandparents believe that there are places like Sumter County all over the world, with great leaders and people who really care. But history unfolds in different ways for different people; and for the people of Americus and Plains, it unfolded in a way that allowed my grandfather to become president of the United States. But I think the same leadership is there in all kinds of small towns all over the place. —Jason Carter

A Habitat homeowner outside her old house

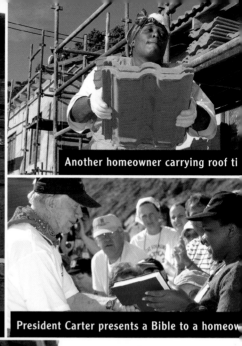
Another homeowner carrying roof ti

President Carter presents a Bible to a homeow

A housekeeper, aided by her employer, paints a window of her new hom

Monica
Sithombana Dlamini
South Africa

and sent missionaries from so many little churches to Africa and sent Grandmama to the Peace Corps. Because of their faith and their history and their understanding of the world, these people decided to help others not just in their own community but around the world. The fact that it all came from little Sumter County is really important to my grandparents."

Like President Carter, actress Jamie Lee Curtis also had a remarkable mother: the movie star Janet Leigh. According to Jamie, her mother grew up in a small town in central California and never forgot her modest roots. When she became successful, she was so grateful that she used her fame to support a number of charities. "When you're a public figure," Jamie says, "you learn quickly that all of the attention you get is useless unless it's turned to the service of others."

Because Janet Leigh's circle of friends included President John F. Kennedy, she became involved with the Special Olympics, founded

> Someone once told me, "Civilization flourishes when great men and women plant trees under the shade of which they will never stand." Those words make more sense to me than all of the yippity-yippity talkity talk that I hear on a daily basis. That people should plant trees under the shade of which they will never stand, or build houses in which they will never live, says it all to me. —Jamie Lee Curtis

THE CARTERS ASKED THEIR GRANDSON JASON to join them at the 2002 Carter Work Project in Durban, South Africa (scenes of which are shown opposite), because Jason had learned to speak Zulu while serving in South Africa for two years as a Peace Corps volunteer. "We went around to all the different houses," Jason remembers, "and my grandfather would say, 'Hi, I'm Jimmy, and this is my grandson.' Then I would translate what he said into Zulu, and people would stand there, literally agape, at the president's grandchild speaking their native language."

by the president's sister Eunice Kennedy Shriver. One day, she took her then thirteen-year-old daughter Jamie with her to volunteer. "It was the first time that I did service on my own," Jamie explains, "and I don't really remember what my job was. But I saw my mother and other celebrities giving out autographs, and I realized that, for a child with mental challenges, an autograph wasn't going to be nearly as meaningful or powerful as a photograph. So, on my own, I lobbied the Polaroid Corporation to donate cameras and film, and the next year I set up a booth, where I was the photographer and the athletes came in to have their picture taken with a celebrity. Those photographs really made a lasting impression on the kids, and the experience made me think, *Oh, not only can I show up, I can also use some of my ideas to make things even better.*"

Good ideas are important, Jamie emphasizes, but if you want to make the ethic of service real, you have to put it into practice. "You've got to live it, breathe it, work it," she says. "And that's why Habitat is so unbelievable, because talk about a lasting impression! You hammer a nail into a piece of wood, and it becomes a house. Talk about feeling like you did something of value, of service to someone else! It's an extraordinarily powerful motivational tool."

Wendy Gabry nails shingles onto a roof.

WENDY GABRY of Lake County, Illinois, signed up for her first Habitat build in 2001. It happened to be sponsored by her church, but, as Wendy says, "If one of the local schools had been

HABITAT'S MONTGOMERY COUNTY, MARYLAND, affiliate encourages children to become involved with the organization by sponsoring an annual LEGO Blitz Build. Working in three-member teams, participants get to design and build model houses out of four hundred LEGO pieces. Entrance fees raise funds for the affiliate.

sponsoring the build, I would have jumped on that one, too, I'm an emergency room nurse, so it's part of my nature to help people."

Wendy had always thought highly of Habitat, and even though she didn't have any previous construction experience, she figured that she could find something useful to do, so she signed up for two days of volunteering. On the first day, which was especially sunny and hot, she worked with the future homeowner, Gloria, nailing

WOMEN BUILD is an increasingly popular Habitat volunteer program for women who want to learn construction skills and build houses on their own. Habitat affiliates across the United States regularly sponsor Women Build projects. When Wendy Gabry took part in the 2007 Carter Work Project in San Pedro, California, she worked on the Women Build house, shown above. Wendy is in the back row, third from the left.

plywood onto what would become the second floor. Both Wendy and Gloria were nervous about climbing up and down the ladder, but they held it steady for each other and worked hard all through the morning and afternoon. Finally, at the end of the day, Wendy asked Gloria for a tour of the property.

"We were both dragging," Wendy remembers, "but Gloria suddenly stood up a little straighter and took me by the arm and walked me around to the front of the house. 'This is my front door,' she said. Then we walked inside, and she said, 'This is my foyer, and this is my kitchen.' We were just looking at two-by-fours that day, but she could already see her future home. She was already envisioning how much better her life would be, and that sold me on Habitat right then."

After those first two days of volunteering, Wendy signed up for several more; and as time passed, she became friendly with three other volunteers. They all started coming once a week on the same day, and eventually they finished Gloria's house. "But we weren't ready yet to give up Habitat," Wendy says. "We'd become kind of addicted to it, so we signed up for another house and began calling ourselves the Habiholics." Now in their ninth year, the Habiholics volunteer every Wednesday, and they've expanded their reach. "As people came along and worked with us, we'd talk to them, and if they expressed some interest, we'd invite them to join our group." As a result, there are now fifteen Habiholics.

Although Wendy has volunteered for other causes, she focuses on Habitat because Habitat "isn't a giveaway program." Instead, it helps people to help themselves. As Wendy explains, "Habitat doesn't just say, 'Okay, we'll all get together and build this house and give it to you.' The homeowners have to show up and get their

Back in the days of the pioneers, families would get together to help one another build barns or houses or whatever else was needed. Those barn raisings always appealed to me, and now I can see why. Working together with other people for a common goal really leaves you with a wonderful feeling of community and connectedness. —Wendy Gabry hands dirty, too. And they've got to pay for the house, which makes it mean so much more to them. Most charities don't do that, which is why Habitat's approach is so novel."

REQUIRING HOMEOWNERS to take an active role isn't the only way in which Habitat differs from most charities. It also asks more of its volunteers. "There's an important difference between volunteering your time and volunteering your money," says Kraig Koschnick. "Giving money is an easy way to say you've done something, but when you only give money, you're not really investing much of yourself or your effort."

A home builder in Bozeman, Montana, Kraig began volunteering with Habitat after his return from a tour of duty in Iraq with the Montana National Guard. "When I started my own business in 2003," Kraig says, "it was my plan to give back to the community through building once a year with Habitat or a similar organization, and in 2004 I signed up for the Jimmy Carter Work Project in Mexico. But about two months later, my National Guard unit was activated, and I was sent to Iraq."

Kraig spent twelve months in Iraq, where he served as a combat medic. "I'll tell you," he says, "Iraq forever changed my

Working as a medic in Iraq, Kraig Koschnick treats a young girl for a burn outside Kirkuk.

Working at the 2008 Carter Work Project in Mississippi, Kraig frames a porch roof.

perception of many, many things—my perception of my country, my perception of the U.S. military, and especially my perception of who I was and who I wanted to be. Iraq really humbled me—all the devastation and poverty I saw over there, the people living with so very little. It broke my heart, to tell you the truth, and it got me really thinking about the pay-it-forward concept. I can't necessarily help those people in Iraq, but I can do something here and hope that, somewhere down the line, someone over there will be able to help them."

Cheboygan, Michigan

Seattle, Washington

Clarksdale, Mississippi

Detroit, Michigan

Maragondon, Philippines

5. How to Build a House

To Habitat volunteers with no previous construction experience—which is almost all of them—a job site can seem disturbingly chaotic at first. But newcomers soon learn that a Habitat project, or build, isn't ordinary chaos; it's highly organized chaos.

On the first rung of the organizational ladder are the rank-and-file volunteers who bring with them, if not building skills, then at least a great deal of energy and enthusiasm. These volunteers are typically divided into crews of three to five people, each supervised by a crew chief.

Crew chiefs are either professional contractors who do construction work for a living or else highly experienced volunteers who have already worked on several Habitat homes, honing their skills. These people direct the work of the rank-and-file volunteers, teaching them what they need to know and working alongside them as they carry out the tasks to which they've been assigned.

Habitat construction sites in the United States and abroad

The crew chiefs, in turn, report to the house leader, who is ultimately in charge of the job site and responsible for everything that goes on there. The house leader schedules the crews, monitors the quality of their work, and makes sure that the workplace is safe.

Although this basic structure holds for all Habitat builds, there are some significant differences in the ways that larger and smaller affiliates operate. According to Russ Griffith, who managed the construction activities of a large affiliate in Nashville before joining Habitat for Humanity International as a construction trainer, the top 10 percent of Habitat affiliates operate like large residential construction companies. "Our affiliate in Bradenton, Florida, for example, knocks out 130 or 140 homes a year," Russ says. "They're well organized, they've got plenty of funding, they've got legions of retired volunteers, and they've got a big paid staff." On the other end of the spectrum, about two-thirds of Habitat's affiliates build just one or two homes a year. These smaller affiliates are mostly staffed by volunteers, and a lot are located in rural areas, where the volunteer pool is limited. "Usually, it's the same group of people week after week after week," Russ continues. "What these smaller affiliates do may not sound like a lot in comparison with the larger affiliates, but you've got to remember that there are a thousand of them, and what they do adds up."

When it comes to training volunteers, smaller affiliates generally make do with on-the-job instruction from crew chiefs, while larger affiliates can afford to offer prebuild classes taught by paid staff. Even so, no matter how well volunteers are trained, inexperienced people tend to make mistakes, so crew chiefs and house leaders have to be watchful. "Quality is extremely important to us and to everyone who works on a house," Russ explains. "Fortunately, as long as the experienced people keep an eye on things, not much can go wrong that isn't easily corrected.

"A classic example of something that crew chiefs have to look out for is problems with the vinyl siding," Russ goes on. "When you're working with vinyl siding, you work up from the bottom of the house, and the new piece is clicked into the piece below it. It's not a difficult step but one that's extremely easy to mess up. You think that it's clicked in, but it isn't, so you get five or six rows up and all of a sudden somebody notices that it's not clicked in. Well, at that point, you can't push it or tug it into place, so you have to take down all of those bad rows and start again. Usually, a good crew chief or house leader will be alert to that, so if it does happen, the crew will have put up only one or two bad rows, which is easy to fix. But I've had days when a crew went all the way to the roof, and we had to back it all off. All you can do then is put a smile on your face and be helpful."

Russ, who grew up in Miami, became involved with Habitat in 1992, when he was living in Nashville and running his own home remodeling business. In September of that year, after Hurricane Andrew devastated much of southern Florida, Russ and his wife went back to Miami to help with the relief effort. "It was such a moving experience," Russ recalls. "My wife and I thought about it and prayed about it, and about a month later, out of

Volunteers hang a row of vinyl siding at the 1998 Carter Work Project in Houston, Texas.

the blue, some Habitat people called me and said, 'We're trying to get this affiliate going. Would you be interested in doing some construction consulting for us?' I said, 'I'll give you one year of my life,' and that was seventeen years ago."

A S WE'VE SEEN, Habitat home designs can take many different forms, and affiliates can run their operations in many different ways, but the actual work involved in constructing a simple, decent home varies very little from job site to job site. That is, all Habitat homes—at least all of them built in the United States—are put together in basically the same way.

The day that volunteers first arrive to begin framing the house is called opening day by many affiliates, but it's never the first day of work. In order to be ready for the volunteers, the affiliate has to prepare the job site. First, of course, it has to acquire the property, select a partner family, and finalize the architectural plans. Then it has to arrange for the foundation to be dug by a professional excavator.

In warmer climates, where the ground doesn't freeze, the excavator needs to dig only deep enough for a simple concrete slab to be poured. The walls of the house are then built directly on top of the slab, although sometimes a raised floor system is added. This creates a crawl space between the floor and the slab, allowing easier access to house systems such as plumbing that run under the floor. In northern climates, where the ground freezes in the winter, the excavator has to extend the foundation below the frost line, which is why nearly all homes in the North have basements. Once concrete is poured to form the basement's floor and walls,

The house wrap covering this wood-framed wall acts as a moisture barrier.

a wooden floor system is added to cover the basement and act as a platform for the rest of the house.

Most Habitat homes built in the United States use wood-frame construction, which means that they are made out of wooden boards. The most common boards are two-by-fours, which are two inches thick by four inches wide when they are first cut from logs. By the time two-by-fours get to a lumberyard, however, they have been dried and planed down, so they measure half an inch less in both thickness and width.

To make the walls of a wood-frame house, volunteers lay out a series of two-by-fours, known as studs, between two parallel two-by-fours, known as plates. Nailing the studs to the plates forms a wall. The studs are usually purchased in eight-foot lengths because standard walls are eight feet high. Plates, on the other hand, are custom cut according to the house plans, because the length of the plate establishes the length of the wall.

VOLUNTEER PHOTOGRAPHER Gregg Pachkowski took this sequence of photos showing the construction of a cement-block house during the 1999 Carter Work Project in the Philippines. Habitat photographer Kim MacDonald took the aerial view of the project site shown below.

"On opening day, if the house needs a floor system, we'll put that in," Russ Griffith explains. "But if we're working with a slab foundation and no crawl space, we'll start right in with the walls, which can be built in two different ways: They can be stick built on the job site, just as carpenters have been doing it for the past two hundred years, or they can be panelized somewhere else and brought to the job site." Panels are studs and plates that have already been nailed together. Sometimes this work is done off-site by volunteers, and sometimes it's done by professionals who are paid by the affiliate, usually at a discounted rate.

"When I was the construction manager in Nashville," Russ continues, "we arranged for a lumber company to build panels for us. We were fortunate because this particular company supported Habitat and didn't charge us for the work. Other large affiliates have warehouses, where volunteers build panels under the supervision of paid staff. The panels are then transported to the job site, where they're erected and nailed together by volunteers. It's like putting together a big jigsaw puzzle. Smaller affiliates, on the other hand, usually build their walls on-site from scratch, which is what we call stick building."

The next step is to sheath the exterior walls. This involves covering the studs and plates with four-by-eight-foot sheets of plywood or a plywood substitute such as oriented strand board (OSB). According to Russ, OSB "looks like a big pile of wood chips that has been run over by a steamroller." Composed of glued-together wood strips, OSB is as strong as plywood but much less costly.

After the sheathing is nailed into place, holes are cut in it for the windows. Meanwhile, another crew begins putting up the roof.

Volunteers deck three roofs during the 1997 Carter Work Project in Pikeville, Kentucky.

Usually, roofs are formed by erecting a series of triangular structures called trusses. The shape of the trusses makes the roof stable by transferring its weight to the house's strong exterior walls. Once the trusses are up, the roof is sheeted, or decked, with plywood or OSB. Then it's covered with black felt, which is thick paper that has been impregnated with asphalt to make it waterproof. (Asphalt is a kind of tar that's also used to pave roads.) "We call this the dry-in stage," Russ says, "because rain can no longer get inside the house."

Once the house is "dried in," the windows and exterior doors are installed, along with a few other outside details—things like gutters to channel rainwater away from the house, porches, and doorbells. The next steps are to side the house and shingle the roof. Larger affiliates with an abundance of volunteers usually undertake

Mowire, Gh

Bunya, Uganda

Urubamba, P

both of these tasks simultaneously, but smaller affiliates will usually do one and then the other.

Meanwhile, other crews can begin working on the interior of the house. The first step there is to use an expanding, weather-resistant foam to seal any places where air might penetrate. "Most important is the gap between the bottom plates and the slab foundation or floor system," Russ says, "but crew chiefs also have to be on the lookout for holes punched into the OSB during the sheathing process or anything like that. The goal is to make the house as airtight as possible, because that way it will be energy efficient."

Once the house is sealed, professionals are brought in to begin installing the electrical, plumbing, and heating and/or cooling systems, because all U.S. building codes require that this work be done by licensed tradespeople. The first stage of the trade work is called roughing in. Electricians will install a master panel and begin running wire through the house, but they won't attach any switches or outlets until the interior walls are covered and painted. Similarly, the plumbers will install the pipes necessary to carry water into the house and sewage out of it, but they won't hook the pipes up to a sink or a toilet until the house is nearly finished.

After the rough-in, volunteers insulate the exterior walls, which means fitting mats of puffy pink fiberglass into the gaps between the studs. (Some northern affiliates use two-by-six studs and plates instead of two-by-fours so that they can use thicker insulation.)

WHEN COMMERCIAL BUILDING MATERIALS aren't available or affordable, Habitat affiliates make their own. Using machines like the one shown opposite (top), local workers press sandy earth into bricks that harden when dried in the hot sun.

Then it's time for the Sheetrock, or drywall. Sheetrock is plaster that has been pressed between two layers of thick paper. It comes in four-foot-wide sheets, just like plywood and OSB, and is used to cover the interior walls of most U.S. buildings.

"Here we get into another difference between larger and smaller affiliates," Russ puts in. "Affiliates building one or two homes a year will generally put up their own drywall, but this can take time. Larger affiliates, which are building many more homes and moving much faster, will usually bring in a drywall professional and let him do it. The difference is that it can take a group of rookie volunteers six or eight weeks to Sheetrock a house. A professional can do the same work better in a day and a half."

Rosalynn Carter nails a sheet of oriented strand board (OSB) to some studs.

Once the drywall is up, the interior painting can begin. When that's done, some types of flooring can go down, and the interior doors and kitchen cabinets can go up. Next comes the trim work. This includes the baseboard, which covers the gaps between the drywall and the flooring; the molding that covers the gaps between the drywall and the ceiling; and the trim that covers the gaps around each window. Meanwhile, the landscaping can get under way—planting the lawn, adding some trees or shrubs, perhaps putting in a driveway.

Finally, the tradespeople come back to do their finish work. "We call what they do at this stage finals or top-outs," Russ says.

"The plumbers will hook up the showers, the faucets, and the toilets, while the electricians install plugs, switches, and lighting fixtures. Then we bring our volunteers back in to clean up and punch out."

Punching out is the last stage of any construction project. It refers to the completion of the punch-out list, which is a list compiled by the house leader of small tasks that were either overlooked in the building process or else done wrong and in need of correction. "The way I used to do it," Russ says, "was to go through the house a couple of days early so that I'd still have volunteers around to help. But my greatest goal has always been to build a house that didn't have any punch-out."

> Generally, if you ask volunteers to put two coats of paint on a house, you'll get six coats because the crews are so enthusiastic. We always get a lot of paint on the houses. —Russ Griffith

WHEN RUSS GRIFFITH was building Habitat houses in Nashville, he moved from opening day to punch-out in just four weekends, which is much quicker than the national average of about four months. "To get houses done in four weekends takes a little more planning," Russ says. "You need to have a lot of material on the job site, ready for volunteers to use, and you need to have a lot of volunteers. Having enough labor means that instead of taking several days to frame a house, we'd typically be shingling the roof by lunchtime on the first day.

"We learned how to work quickly," Russ explains, "because the four-weekend schedule suited our house sponsors. These were large organizations, often churches, and they had very full outreach programs. Long-term commitments were difficult for them, but they could easily deliver a large number of volunteers for four consecutive weekends. A lot of other affiliates soon adopted our schedule because building houses quickly is more satisfying and more exciting.

"Part of my job now," Russ continues, "is to go around the country and talk to different affiliates about their building practices. Often they'll say to me, 'You know, it takes us thirty-three weeks to build a house, and we've run out of volunteers.' And my answer is, 'I'm not surprised. Your volunteers are probably bored to death.' On the other hand, if you build a house in four weekends, at the end of the first weekend you're already 25 percent done, and the volunteers go home saying, 'Look here! I built a house today!' That fires them up, and they can't wait to come back."

The Habitat term for this type of accelerated schedule is a blitz build, and Lynchburg, Virginia, contractor Tom Gerdy is an expert at them. Tom began working with Habitat in the late 1980s after he was approached by leaders of the new Lynchburg affiliate. They asked him to serve on the board of directors, but he declined because he doesn't see himself as a "board-type" person. "I don't do well in committee meetings," Tom says. "But I told them that for anything hands on, I was there." So he began working on the affiliate's first house, and he has been hooked ever since.

What's It For? *A miter (or chop) saw is great for cutting studs and plates because two-by-fours can easily be laid across its stationary base. Cutting a sheet material like plywood, however, requires a handheld circular saw that can travel across the board.*

"Back in those days," Tom says, "my focus was a little bit twisted. I thought that making a dollar was pretty important. But once I got to spend some time with Habitat, I learned quickly that chasing the dollar doesn't bring happiness. Creating happiness for other people is what you want to be doing. It has certainly worked out for me, and I still thank the people who invited me in."

According to Tom, his most useful skill as a blitz build leader is his ability to visualize all the processes that go into house building. He then breaks those processes down into small steps that nearly anyone can accomplish. That way, people without any skills can still join in the build and participate effectively. "Now," Tom says, "we've gotten to the point where we can take a couple of hundred people, only a few of whom have trade skills, and put together a house in a couple of days."

Tom Gerdy oversees a September 2005 build in Burbank, California. The house, when finished, was shipped to Louisiana for use by victims of Hurricane Katrina.

Tom has had a lot of practice at blitz building because in 1998 he founded a group that calls itself the Habitat Road Trip Crazies. "During the early days in Lynchburg, people from around the region heard what we were doing and came to help us," Tom explains. "Soon, Lynchburg became one of the top affiliates. But after about ten years, some of us decided that we needed to pay all that help forward, so we started going on the road to help smaller affiliates generate the same excitement we had here."

Volunteers scramble to fini

The new homeowners celebra

The first Road Trip Crazies were about twenty of Tom's friends from Lynchburg. But as the group has traveled around the country, its size has grown. In 2007, eighty-three Crazies from thirteen different states showed up for a blitz build in Ohio. The following year, seventy-six Crazies from twelve different states took part in a similar blitz build in North Carolina. The energy and excitement that the Crazies bring to each of their builds inspires local people to join them, often in large numbers.

The Crazies' goal is to get people who have thought about volunteering to take the first step. As Tom says, "People want to feel that they were put here for a reason, that they can make a difference. The problem is they don't have the confidence to take that first step. They don't know how to jump through that first hoop to get started. What our group does is make that first step easy.

"What we've found," Tom continues, "is that a blitz build is an excellent way to stir up a community, and we really market these things hard." The Crazies will usually begin working with an affiliate two or even three months in advance of a build. In order to generate publicity, Tom will teach the affiliate how to place stories in the local media and how to get people talking about the project. "Some people at an affiliate on Virginia's eastern shore once told me that on their best days, they got only twenty volunteers," Tom recalls. "So I told them, 'Okay, we're going to create an event. You're going

ON DECEMBER 17, 2002, Habitat for Humanity of Shelby County (Alabama) built a house in three hours, twenty-six minutes, and forty-six seconds. Their effort set a new record for the fastest-built Habitat house — eclipsing the previous record of three hours, forty-four minutes, and fifty-nine seconds held by Habitat for Humanity New Zealand.

to get the local newspaper to do an article six weeks in advance of the build, and then you're going to get the paper to do a follow-up story about three weeks before, when your foundation's going in. Then you're going to arrange for the local radio station to do a live remote from the job site, and you're going to do radio and television interviews.'" On the first day of that weekend blitz build, 175 people showed up. On the final day, a Monday, when people were already getting back to work, there were still 75 volunteers. Meanwhile, two houses had been framed, sided, shingled, and Sheetrocked.

But where the houses end up, Tom says, isn't really as important as the number of people—religious or not—who come out and "feel the feeling." This is Habitat speak for the sensation that people get when they come to realize that their efforts really can make the world a better place. "It's letting your heart tell your hands what to do," Tom explains, "and there's an immediate gratification that comes from working hand in hand with other good people who all understand what is really important. We don't get a lot of years on this earth, and the sooner we learn that looking after each other is the answer, the better off everybody will be."

Of all of Tom's stories, the one he most enjoys telling concerns his "rooftop revelation." The story begins with a phone call from a Jewish friend whose synagogue wants to build a Habitat house. The problem is that the Lynchburg affiliate schedules most of its work on Saturdays, which is the Jewish Sabbath and thus a day on which observant Jews are not allowed to work. Tom's friend needed to find an experienced builder willing to lead the synagogue group on a Sunday build, and Tom agreed. "I don't do too well sitting in a pew, so I welcomed the chance to do my praying with a hammer in my hand," Tom says. The framing took place on Palm Sunday, and at the end of the day, Tom found himself up on the roof, supervising the decking. "We'd had a great day, and I was standing on the ridge of the roof with the sun going down when it hit me. Here I was, a lapsed Catholic who now attends a United Methodist church, working with a Christian organization on a home sponsored by a Jewish synagogue for a family of Baptists. At that moment, I realized that no matter what your vision of a supreme being may be, this is what he or she had in mind. We're all just supposed to join hands and do what's needed.

I've had plenty of people walk away from one of our events and tell me that they feel guilty because their hope was to give to somebody else and instead they got more than they gave. For twenty years now, I've been trying to give more than I receive, but I haven't been able to accomplish it, either. —Tom Gerdy

"I'm a believer that, no matter what challenges we face, we have the answers," Tom continues. "We spend a lot of time looking to government and to other people for the answers, but all we really have to do is look inside ourselves. We can solve the problems. We can solve them all. It just takes people listening to their hearts and being passionate. Passionate people like that can change the world in a hurry, and that's what we've been trying to do."

As GROUPS OF HABITAT VOLUNTEERS like the Road Trip Crazies work together again and again, they develop job site traditions that take on great meaning for them. On the builds that Russ Griffith supervised, all of the volunteers would sign a large piece of vinyl, some adding personal messages or quotations from Scripture.

Tom Gerdy, wearing his signature hardhat, instructs volunteers at a blitz build.

"We'd roll it up, put a big rubber band around it, and present it to the family at the dedication of their house, for posterity's sake," Russ says.

A much more common practice is to sign the house itself. The Crazies do this once the framing is complete. According to Tom Gerdy, "We stop the entire site and say, 'Okay, we need to take a moment here, because the partner family is going to be living in this house for a long time, and no doubt there will be some tough times ahead. Because you're out here giving your blood, sweat, and tears to help this family build their home, we want you to sign this house to show the family that no matter what they may face, there will always be the good wishes of two or three hundred people here with them, helping them find peace and happiness in this home.'"

The volunteers who worked on Dawn Stolz's Habitat house in Bay St. Louis, Mississippi, developed their own unusual take on this tradition. Dawn is a single mother whose house in Waveland (the town next door to Bay St. Louis) was destroyed by Hurricane

Katrina in August 2005. "When my son and I heard that the hurricane was coming, we drove about an hour and a half north to Collins, Mississippi, where my cousin lives," Dawn recalls. "When the storm was over, I came back to see what had happened. I got home around midnight and learned that there wasn't any home left to come back to." It wasn't until the next morning that Dawn found her roof, which had been ripped off her house by the wind and carried about a football field away.

For a month Dawn and her thirteen-year-old son, Nico, lived with her brother, then she moved into a trailer provided by the Federal Emergency Management Agency (FEMA). But formaldehyde in the trailer produced fumes that gave Nico breathing problems. Fortunately, Dawn's parents owned a nearby rental property. It had also been damaged by the hurricane, but as soon as two bedrooms and a bathroom were repaired, Dawn and Nico moved in. That solution was only temporary, however.

Although Dawn's insurance paid off her mortgage on the house that was destroyed, she had nothing left over to put toward a new house. Meanwhile, she and Nico had lost all of their belongings. "I was so whipped after the storm that I thought I'd never be a home-owner again," Dawn says. But Dawn's father, who often volunteers with Habitat, suggested that she apply for a Habitat home. At the time, the closest affiliate was in Jackson, the Mississippi state capital. But as Habitat mobilized its resources in response to the disaster on the Gulf Coast, a new affiliate was formed in Hancock County, where Dawn was living. Habitat for Humanity Bay-Waveland Area took over her application, sent a social worker to conduct a home

Pittsburgh, Pennsylvania

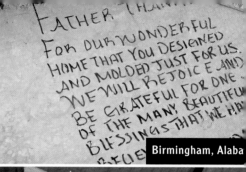

FATHER THAN...
FOR OUR WONDERFUL
HOME THAT YOU DESIGNED
AND MOLDED JUST FOR US.
WE WILL REJOICE AND
BE GRATEFUL FOR ONE
OF THE MANY BEAUTIFUL
BLESSINGS THAT WE HA...

Birmingham, Alaba...

May
this house
provide the
foundation
for generation
of love,
security,
and family...

Americorps
NCCC
2008

Biloxi, Mississippi

Violet, Louisia...

MAY THE
LORD BLESS
You & KEEP
You.

Violet, Louisiana

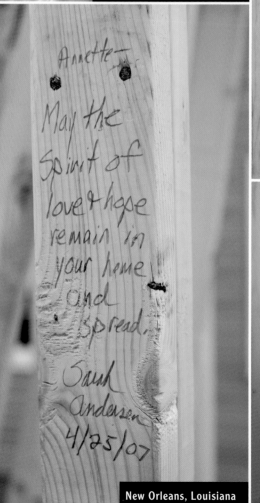

Annette—

May the
Spirit of
love & hope
remain in
your home
and
spread.

— Sarah
Andersen
4/25/07

New Orleans, Louisiana

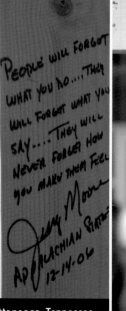

PEOPLE WILL FORGOT
WHAT YOU DO....THEY
WILL FORGOT WHAT YOU
SAY....THEY WILL
NEVER FORGET HOW
YOU MAKE THEM FEEL

Jerry Moore
AP APPALACHIAN SERVICE
12-14-06

Chattanooga, Tennessee

Welcome Home !!!
Dave Connier

Memphis, Tenness...

visit, and soon approved Dawn and Nico as a partner family. Their new house, completed in February 2007, was the fourth Habitat home built by the Bay-Waveland affiliate. Two years later, the affiliate completed its one-hundredth house.

Dawn's house was sponsored by the Willow Creek Church of South Barrington, Illinois, which is about a thousand miles away from Bay St. Louis. In addition to donating the money to finance the house, the church sent members down to help with the construction. "When they arrived," Dawn recalls, "they told me about a group of church members who couldn't make the trip but still wanted to be a part of my house. They showed me little slips of paper on which these people had written some prayers, and they asked if it would be okay if they nailed these slips of paper inside the walls of my house.

"After the house was finished," Dawn continues, "I hosted a women's Bible group here, and we were sitting around the room, talking, when I said, 'Do y'all know that this is a Habitat home?' And not everyone did, so I told them about the group from Willow Creek Church that had helped build the house and about how the people who couldn't come put their prayers on those slips of paper, and how we nailed them inside the

Dawn Stoltz poses in front of her new Habitat home during the 2006 Bay St. Louis blitz build.

walls. I told the group that we were surrounded by prayers, and everybody in the room went 'Oooooh,' and one lady said, 'I've got chill bumps!'"

HANDWRITTEN MESSAGES
LEFT BY HABITAT VOLUNTEERS

Miami, Florida

Pascagoula, Mississ

Baltimore, Maryland

Anniston, Alabama

Benton Harbor, Michig

Pensacola, Florida

Lilongwe, Mala

6. Bridge-Building

H ABITAT FOR HUMANITY doesn't just build houses. It also builds bridges between people—bridges between volunteers and partner families, between volunteers and other volunteers, and even between celebrities and people who aren't well known outside their own families.

Brothers Sherwood and Dale Kirk are Habitat volunteers who have built more than their share of homes and bridges. The Kirks grew up in western Kentucky, where Dale went to work for a large commercial builder and Sherwood went into education, first as a junior high school teacher and then as an administrator.

During the early 1990s, while working in Owensboro, Dale heard Millard Fuller speak about Habitat. "He was a super-interesting guy and so outgoing," Dale recalls. "If he met you just once, he'd remember your name. How he did that, I don't know, but he was pretty good at it." Dale was impressed with what Fuller had to say, but his work life kept him too busy to follow up. In 1998, however, Dale's marriage ended, and his life began to change.

HABITAT PARTNER FAMILIES AND VOLUNTEERS
WORKING TOGETHER AT HOME AND FAR AWAY

Dilapidated housing in Cabresti, Romania, a village next to Beius

To get away for a while, he went down to Americus, Georgia, where a boyhood friend had become principal of the local high school. Dale's plan was to spend a few months helping his friend build a new house; but while he was there, remembering his encounter with Fuller, he stopped into Habitat's international headquarters on Lamar Street. Soon, Dale signed up for a blitz build just north of town. It was part of Fuller's plan to get rid of all the poverty housing in Sumter County. At that Easter 1999 build, Dale met Doug Dahlgren, a Habitat construction consultant stationed in Budapest, Hungary.

"Doug was recruiting people for a ten-house blitz build in Beius, Romania," Dale remembers, "and he was such a good salesman that before I knew it, I had agreed to become the construction director."

Dale didn't really know what he was getting himself into, but he soon found out. For one thing, the national affiliate in Romania was still very new, so volunteers were scarce; and for another, Romanians didn't known much about wood-frame construction because they built most of their houses out of concrete blocks. Even so, Dale made things work.

"I went to Romania for three months to do the prebuild," he explains. "We got all the slabs poured, prebuilt all the trusses, and arranged to have all the materials on-site for the blitz. Then in the fall I went back for a second build and stayed on for another month to teach classes on wood-frame construction. I'd teach in the office for a couple of hours, and then we'd go out on a job site and apply what we had talked about."

Dale worked with a number of different partner families in Beius, including the Lucans—whose eighteen-year-old daughter, Monica, spoke English well and sometimes acted as Dale's translator. Because the Lucans hadn't been able to afford a house of their own, they had been living with Monica's grandmother. "Her house was old, small, and dark," Monica says. "I

Children play in front of their family's new Habitat home in Beius.

remember that I hated rain because the roof had cracks in it, and every time it rained, water would pour in all over the house. I was very ashamed of where I lived, and I never invited my friends over because I worried that they might laugh."

ADRIAN CIORNA, now the national director of Habitat for Humanity Romania, first came into contact with Habitat through Good Samaritan, an organization he founded to help Romanian orphans. Through Ciorna's efforts, Habitat Romania found a useful source of inexpensive labor, and the orphans learned skills that could help them get construction jobs.

The house was so small, in fact, that Monica had to share a room—and a bed—with her grandmother. "You can imagine how I felt," she says. "I read in bed a lot because I really enjoyed reading. But my grandmother would always be asking me to turn off the light so that she could sleep. All I really wanted was to have something that was mine—a room, a house—and not to be ashamed of it."

Having heard about Habitat from a friend, Monica urged her parents to apply for a house. At first, they were afraid, worrying that they couldn't afford the mortgage payments. "But I insisted," Monica says, "and I convinced my father, who started volunteering with me. Because he was something of a dreamer, people in town said he wasn't serious. But he was, and he came with me often to the Habitat site, where we met Mr. Dale. Eventually, Habitat accepted our application, and Mr. Dale helped us build a house on a field that my grandmother had donated to Habitat."

The Lucans moved into their new home not long after Monica turned nineteen. It was a very happy day, but the family still had some problems to work through. When Monica was eighteen, she had applied to college and had been accepted, but she wasn't able to go because her parents couldn't afford the tuition. When she was nineteen, she applied again and was accepted again, but she still didn't know where the tuition money would come from. "My mother would cry but not in joy," Monica says. "She cried in anger and said, 'Oh, my God, what are we going to do? We don't have the money for you. We don't have the money to pay for the house.' So she was upset, and I was upset, and that's the time when Sherwood and Marsha came to Romania."

AFTER RETURNING FROM BEIUS in the fall of 1999, Dale Kirk found out that he had contracted Habititis. "It's the disease you get when you're hooked on Habitat," Dale says—and he was certainly hooked. In 2000, working with Doug Dahlgren again, he spent five months in Braga, Portugal, consulting on a Global Village build. (Through the Global Village program, Habitat volunteers build houses in parts of the world unfamiliar to them while learning about the host country's culture.)

While Dale was in Portugal, he e-mailed his brother Sherwood regularly, encouraging him to come over. "Sherwood kept telling me that he and his wife, Marsha, were coming," Dale says. "But it was getting close to the end of my stay, and finally I said, 'Look, if you're gonna come, it had better be soon, because I'll be home in a month.'"

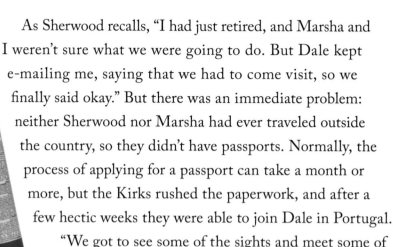

As Sherwood recalls, "I had just retired, and Marsha and I weren't sure what we were going to do. But Dale kept e-mailing me, saying that we had to come visit, so we finally said okay." But there was an immediate problem: neither Sherwood nor Marsha had ever traveled outside the country, so they didn't have passports. Normally, the process of applying for a passport can take a month or more, but the Kirks rushed the paperwork, and after a few hectic weeks they were able to join Dale in Portugal.

"We got to see some of the sights and meet some of the Global Village teams that Dale was working with," Sherwood says. "But all the time we were there, Dale kept saying that he wanted to go back to Romania to show us where he had built the year before."

What's It For? *Caulk is a waterproof gel used to seal gaps, especially around bathroom and kitchen fixtures. Pulling the trigger of a caulking gun forces a thin bead of caulk out of the replaceable tube.*

They flew to Budapest, rented a car, and drove to Beius. "At that time, Marsha and I still weren't sold on Habitat. We thought that the volunteers were probably just do-gooders trying to show off or something," Sherwood explains. "But when we got to Beius, we saw all these people running up to Dale on the street, shouting, 'Mr. Dale! Mr. Dale!' And they would have one of two reactions: either they would start crying on the spot or else they would run up to him and give him a big hug. I'd never seen that kind of outpouring of emotion before. You could really tell how much he had influenced their lives and how much they cared for him. So Marsha and I started thinking, 'Well, there might be something to this Habitat thing.'"

While Dale caught up with his friends in Beius, Sherwood and Marsha toured the town in the company of Monica Lucan, whom Dale had asked to serve as their translator. Monica was working in a sewing factory at the time—"kind of a sweatshop," according to Sherwood—to help her parents pay the mortgage on their Habitat house. "She was so intelligent," Marsha recalls, "that we had to ask her why she wasn't going to college, and she said that her grades were good enough, but she couldn't afford it. Then I asked her how much college would cost, and she said about $350 a year. So I told Sherwood, 'Give me the checkbook!'"

That trip to Romania in the late summer of 2000 began what Sherwood calls "a whirlwind." By the time he and Marsha got back to Kentucky, they had both contracted bad cases of Habititis. Right away, they signed up for the 2000 Carter Work Project in Jacksonville, Florida, even though its start date was a week away and they had only just returned from Europe. "We went to Jacksonville," Sherwood remembers, "and the people there, the friends we made, said, 'Hey, you going with the build next year?' And we go, 'Well, where's the build next year?' And they go, 'Uh, South Korea.' And we go, *'South Korea?'* I mean, who goes to *South Korea* for a vacation? But, listen, we went and we *loved* it. It was *fabulous*."

I don't have a lot of self-confidence, so when I first started volunteering, I thought, *Oh, I can't do this. I don't have any skills.* But on our first build, this fellow took me under his wing and said, "You're going up on the roof. And I said, "No, I'm not." But he insisted, and he helped me get upstairs and climb through the window. On the roof, volunteers were nailing down shingles, and the men were breaking them because they were hitting them too hard. So I started tap-tap-tapping, and I did two rows without breaking a single one, and I thought, *Okay, I really can contribute.* —Marsha Kirk

Not only did Sherwood and Marsha go to the Carter Work Project in South Korea in 2001 (with Dale acting as construction director), they also took part in the Carter Work Projects in South Africa in 2002, Alabama in 2003, Mexico in 2004, Michigan in 2005, India in 2006, Los Angeles in

Monica Lucan (left) with Marsha Kirk during the Kirks' 2004 trip to Beius

2007, and the Gulf Coast in 2008. In the meantime, they began volunteering for Global Village builds. Their first took them to Northern Ireland, and then in early 2004, Marsha saw that a Global Village build was being planned for April in Beius.

"Monica was graduating from college in June of that year, so we decided to go and see her," Sherwood says. "We got to meet her fiancé on that trip, and she invited us over for dinner so many times that the rest of the team started calling us the socialites of Beius."

The following spring, Marsha received an e-mail from Monica with an important request. She wanted to know whether Sherwood and Marsha would come back to Beius in July to give her away at her wedding. According to Sherwood, Marsha said, "Get the tickets. We're going!"

"Here was a person whom we met through Habitat, whose family lived in a Habitat house," Sherwood says. "We changed her life, and being able to do that changed ours, too. She's now a teacher, her husband is a teacher, and she never would have had the opportunity to do that if she were still working in the sewing factory in Beius."

S HERWOOD AND MARSHA'S EXPERIENCE illustrates a point that Danielle Weir makes about interacting with people in need. "Something I learned when I was young and have relearned in my nonprofit work is the importance of inviting the poor to a sense of dignity," Danielle says. "Habitat does that by inviting people to participate in the building of their own home. It'd certainly be easier to have professional builders do all the work and not get involved with homeowners and volunteers, but Habitat is about more than just the physical outcome. It's about the process, and part of that process is creating dignity in the lives of the partner families. Another part is having everyday people come out to help. All of it is connected."

Valerie Bean is another volunteer who has been able to build homes and bridges. Her connection to Habitat comes through the Carter family. Although she now lives in suburban Atlanta, Valerie grew up in Americus, where as a teenager she was friendly with the president's sister Gloria and her kids. Years later, however, she ran into the president's son Jeff at a youth soccer game in which they both had children playing. "It turns out that he had just moved in down the street from me," Valerie remembers. "And he said, 'Oh, my gosh,' and I said, 'Oh, my gosh,' and we've been best friends ever since."

As Valerie got to know Jeff better, she became friendly with his parents as well. "President and Mrs. Carter just took me in like I was one of their own," Valerie says.

> My life has changed very much since I met Marsha and Sherwood. I call Marsha my second mother. She has helped me with much more than just money. She came to my wedding. She came to visit me after I gave birth to my baby boy, and she supported me in so many other ways. When I'm down, she tells me, "You're okay, you're strong, you can do this." —Monica Lucan

"He especially liked that I was willing to argue with him. He's so used to people saying, 'Yes, sir. Yes, sir. Yes, sir,' and although I respect that big time, he knows that if he fusses with me, I'll give it right back to him."

In March 1999, about three years after Valerie reconnected with Jeff, she got a phone call from Jeff's wife, Annette. "Oh, we're going to the Philippines for this year's work project," Annette said — knowing that Valerie had once worked in the Philippines and could speak Tagalog, the Filipino national language. "You've got to come with us."

Having grown up in Americus, Valerie knew all about Habitat, of course, and even considered Millard Fuller to be one of her mentors, but she had never taken part in a build before. "I said, 'Okay, I'll go. When is it?' And Annette said, 'It's in two weeks.' And I'm, like, 'What! Two weeks!' But I got it together and went because the Filipino people had taken such good care of me when I was there, and I wanted to give something back."

Valerie Bean (far right) with her crew in front of the completed Bocalan house

The homeowners on whose house Valerie and the Carters worked were Emma and Florencio Bocalan. Before moving into their Habitat house, the Bocalans lived in an abandoned septic tank. "It was a large concrete rectangle," Valerie says, "not really a house but a shelter. They mostly lived outside it but used it as a place to crawl into and sleep at night. They also kept their possessions in it, mostly just pots and pans."

The house that Valerie helped to build out of concrete blocks had no indoor plumbing, no separate rooms, and measured only three hundred square feet. "It looked just like a room you or I would build to put our riding lawn mower in," Valerie says. "We used eight-by-ten sheets of plywood to divide off some sleeping areas, and that was about it. But to Emma and Florencio, who had been living in a septic tank, it was a mansion."

Embarrassed by their poverty, the Bocalans and their children didn't say much. "But when they found out that I spoke Tagalog and knew the local customs," Valerie says, "I became their angel. Emma especially clung to me all week because I was a little more familiar than the other volunteers, but still she didn't say a word."

One of the Bocalans' children draws on the floor of his family's new Habitat house.

Finally, on the last day of the blitz build, a local television crew showed up at the Carter house to tape some interviews. According to Valerie, the young reporter was obviously the daughter of a wealthy family and therefore hadn't had much contact with poor Filipinos. ("When I lived in the Philippines," Valerie says, "my wealthy friends really didn't know much or care much about the lower economic classes.")

As Valerie tells the story, "This young woman asked Emma how she felt owning a Habitat house, and Emma stood up boldly and said in Tagalog, 'You know what? I was a poor washerwoman, and people said to me, "You'll never have a home, and your kids will never go to school, because you're just a poor washerwoman.'" Then she paused and said, 'Now look at my beautiful home. *Look at my beautiful home!*' And all the pride in her heart came out because she knew that her children would now be able to go to school and have a safe home and a safe playground, which were things that they'd never had.

"Well, I started crying," Valerie continues, "and I looked over at the reporter, and she was crying, too. And she looked at me, and she asked, 'Did you understand what she said?' And I said, 'Yes.' But the other people in the room didn't know yet because none of them spoke Tagalog."

That night at the closing ceremonies, the same reporter went up on stage to make some introductions, but in the middle she stopped herself and said, "I want to take a minute to talk to you about the Filipino people. We are a wonderful people in many ways, but we don't give as much as we should. Today, I had an experience that changed my life forever. Until today, I hadn't realized how easy it is to give and what giving means to people. So I'm going to make a pledge to you right now that I'm changing my life and I'm going to care." Hearing that short speech,

The young reporter who was touched by Emma Bocalan's words interviews Rosalynn Carter.

Valerie began to cry again. "I knew what had happened to her," Valerie explains. "I had seen her face, and I knew that what Emma had said really had changed her life."

"That week restored my faith in mankind," Valerie Bean says. "People really are good. They just need a reason, a chance, to go out and show how good they are." Not surprisingly, Valerie came down with her own case of Habititis. Although soccer leagues and school activities keep her busy most of the year, she still sets aside at least one week for the annual Carter Work Project. Over time, she has both moved up to crew chief and become friendly with the Kirks.

In 2002, when Dale Kirk was masterminding the prebuild for the Carter Work Project in Durban, South Africa, he sent Sherwood an e-mail, letting his brother know that Dale was making him chief of the roofing crew on the Carter house. At first, Sherwood objected. "I don't want to be a chief," he told Dale. "I just want to be an Indian." But Dale wrote back that he needed to have someone he could trust on the job, so Sherwood relented—and that's how Sherwood and Marsha became regulars on the Carter house and got to know Valerie.

I F YOU TALK TO ENOUGH HABITAT REGULARS, you'll find that they often speak of themselves as a fraternity or sorority; and like old college classmates, they enjoy getting together. "It's certainly a great reunion for Rosalynn and me," President Carter agrees, "because so many of the same volunteers show up year after year after year—some of them for twenty-five years—and the only time we get to see them is when we come back for Habitat."

Yet new volunteers rarely feel like outsiders. "When I went to Los Angeles and New Orleans for the 2007 and 2008 Carter builds, another Habiholic went with me, so I had a friend there,"

VOLUNTEERS WHO TAKE PART in Habitat for Humanity's Global Village program get to experience foreign cultures in a way that visitors rarely do. Combining service with tourism, they work alongside members of the host community, learning about the local people as they help them build simple, decent homes for themselves. The Global Village team shown here is helping local volunteers move bricks to a Habitat build site in Urubamba, Peru.

Wendy Gabry says. "But I would have gone even if I didn't have a friend with me because when you're on a job site, you make a million new friends. The reason is that everyone's there to help each other. I know this, and somebody else knows that, and we all get it done by working together."

Kraig Koschnick had a similar experience. "After I got back from Iraq, I found out that there was a Habitat essay contest, and because I enjoy writing, I entered it," Kraig says. "I ended up winning the contest, and my prize was a trip to the 2008 Carter

Work Project in Mississippi. I was ecstatic about going, and I thought I would just help wherever they needed me, but when I got there, I found out that I had been assigned to Jimmy Carter's house, and that's where I met Sherwood and Marsha. Going to Mississippi by myself, not having any experience, not knowing anybody there, I was really fortunate to have Sherwood take me under his wing, and we became pretty inseparable, just sharing stories and laughing and enjoying what we were doing. Since then, we've stayed in touch, and I can't wait to see them again at this year's build."

I've built houses for a living for thirteen years, mostly for very wealthy people, and some of those houses have cost millions of dollars. But the irony is that I'm not sure I ever built a *home* until I built one with Habitat for Humanity. It was a wonderful, humbling experience, and I can't wait to do it again.
—Kraig Koschnick

Like the Carters, some of the volunteers at Habitat builds are quite well known. "We get to see a lot of celebrities," Sherwood says. "Marsha even got to work with Brad Pitt in India. But one thing you have to learn is that you need to check your ego at the door. On a Habitat site, we're all on the same level with just one purpose in mind. Who you are or what you do for a living doesn't matter. Whether you're an engineer or an actor or a CEO, if somebody's a little better than you, you let them take the lead."

A story that Marsha tells about the 2008 Carter Work Project on the Gulf Coast illustrates Sherwood's point. "I was working with the former president of Romania," she says, "and he kept taking the paint roller and accidentally hitting the ceiling with it. I didn't have the nerve to tell him he was messing up, so I got someone else to do it. But he was such a gentleman about it that

Trisha Yearwood paints a window frame during the 2007 Carter Work Project.

I could have told him myself. Later, I got to telling him about my friendship with Monica and how much I loved his country. So at the end of the week, he brought two books that he had written to the site, and he inscribed them. One he gave to President Carter, and one he gave to me."

Other well-known Habitat regulars include the country singers Garth Brooks and Trisha Yearwood, who happen to be married to each other. "You remember how I was saying that President Carter is really nice?" Valerie Bean smiles. "Well, you wouldn't believe how wonderful Garth and Trisha are. I remember one day in Mississippi, Trisha and Garth were supposed to leave no later than two o'clock to travel to a country music event in another city. But Garth was helping my husband on the roof, and when two o'clock came around, Garth said, 'We're not leaving until this job is done,' which wasn't until five o'clock."

Garth and Trisha became interested in Habitat for several different reasons. "For me," says Trisha, who's from Georgia, "it was knowing that the Carters were involved. Habitat was something that was always on my radar, and when Garth and I were invited to do a build, we went, and I fell in love. It's amazing how much satisfaction you get doing the work and learning the ins and outs of Habitat—how the homeowners are so involved, how hard they work to get their homes, and how much pride they take in them."

For Garth, the road to Habitat began at the 2007 National Hockey League All-Star Game in Dallas, where he met Habitat director of special initiatives Karen Haycox. "I live my life through whatever you want to call it—karma, divine intervention, whatever," Garth says. "And I met Karen out in the parking lot, and she kind of roped me in. No choice. I had to work with her. But I've got to tell you that Habitat has been one of the greatest things that has ever happened to me. Building with the homeowner is my favorite part. The whole day goes by, and if you're outside, you're a fried lobster by the time it's over, but you still don't want to leave. You've made all these new relationships, and you just want to keep building.

My favorite thing to do on a Habitat job site is to hammer. Maybe I'm just taking out aggression, but I like to swing the hammer. It makes me happy. And the thing I like to do least is quit at the end of the day. I don't like to be done. —Trisha Yearwood

Garth Brooks checks whether a line is level.

"Charity brings you two things," Garth continues. "It brings you the feeling of a gift, and it also brings you a feeling of guilt because you don't know how to repay what you've been given. Well, that's not what Habitat does. Habitat teaches people to earn something for themselves so that, by the time they move into the house, instead of feeling guilt, they're filled with pride. They feel they've done this for themselves—and the truth is, they have."

Orange Farm, South Africa

Jamaica

Old Offinso, Gh

TOILET   BATH-ROOM   KITCHEN

Buoyem, Ghana

Rewari, In

Khao Lak, Thailand

Sen Sok, Cambodia

Mzuzu, Mala

7. How to Install a Toilet

A HUMAN NEED even more basic than the need for shelter is the need for water. Humans can't live without it. Yet clean, readily available drinking water is beyond the daily grasp of more than one billion people worldwide. Therefore—in order to build simple, decent homes for low-income people—Habitat has had to pay increasingly close attention to the related issues of water and sanitation.

When planners speak of water, they mean the dependable delivery of safe drinking water to a home. When they speak of sanitation, they mean the safe removal of human waste from a home.

"We have always been involved in water and sanitation at the household level," Steve Weir explains. "But as our programs have grown in size, we've found that we're having to add a community-wide water-sanitation component that we didn't have to worry about in the early years. Now water and sanitation are huge considerations for us."

EXAMPLES OF WATER AND SANITATION
FACILITIES AROUND THE WORLD

According to Steve, Habitat's biggest concern in rural areas is water quality. Because rural areas are too sparsely populated to make public water systems worthwhile, rural communities typically rely on drilled or dug wells. But wells are not always safe. "It depends on the soil and how deep the groundwater is," Steve says. "In Bangladesh, for example, the soil contains a lot of arsenic, which is a poison. So a well drilled in Bangladesh can actually supply poisoned water."

Poor sanitation practices also affect water quality. "In some parts of the world, where sanitation isn't well understood, waste systems are sometimes placed close to wells," Steve says. "If they're placed too close, waste can drain into a well, causing a lot of health problems."

In urban areas, on the other hand, the main water problem is access. Although utilities have plenty of water to sell, they're reluctant to offer service in low-income or slum areas because they're worried about getting paid. They fear that customers with legal water connections won't pay regularly and that other residents who connect illegally (a practice known as pirating) won't pay at all. "The problem that water companies face, if they agree to deliver metered water to you," Steve explains, "is that before the water gets to you, six other families up the line have already tapped into it illegally. That makes serving you a bad deal for the water company."

One of the strategies that Habitat has pursued to solve this problem is called secondary piping. First, Habitat persuades the utility to run a water line to the edge of the community, where a single meter is installed. Then, with Habitat's help, partner families

IN POOR RURAL AREAS of the world, waterways are commonly used as toilets. This photograph shows a riverside toilet near a Habitat building site in Minh Hoa, Vietnam. The houses being built there by Habitat for Humanity Vietnam will all have enclosed toilets.

run secondary piping to their individual homes. Sometimes, they install submeters to keep track of usage; otherwise, they simply divide the monthly bill equally among the connected families.

"It's a great deal for the water companies," Steve says. "No piracy, no collection issues, and the utility doesn't even have to maintain the secondary piping. It's also a great deal for the residents. Even though they have to pay for the secondary piping, the fees charged by the water company are less than half the cost of having water trucked in or buying it bottled. It's actually a great deal for everyone involved."

IN RURAL VARJADA, BRAZIL, Habitat's innovative rooftop rain-water collection systems have solved the water delivery problem, but water quality remains a concern because rainwater stored in an

outdoor cistern is not necessarily safe to drink. In order to make it safe, homeowners have to treat the water with chemicals and then pass it through a filter. Untreated water is safe only for bathing, washing up, and filling the tank of each home's indoor flush toilet.

Sanitation in Varjada is handled with septic systems. When a toilet is flushed, the water carries the waste from the toilet into an underground septic tank. There, the waste settles to the bottom of the tank while excess water percolates into the surrounding soil. Every so often, a truck equipped with a large pump empties the tank and transports the waste to a disposal site.

In some places, however, where outdoor toilets are the cultural norm and indoor toilets are considered bizarre, Habitat designers plan accordingly. The most common alternative is the composting toilet, an outhouse-like structure that sits on top of one or more holes in the ground. "The simplest model is the two-seater," Steve Weir says. "When one side fills up, you just throw some enzymes into the hole and switch seats. Over time, the enzymes break down the waste in that hole and turn it into fertilizer." Then the fertilizer is scooped out, the seats are switched, and the process starts all over again.

In urban areas, most Habitat homes have indoor toilets. But in some countries, it's not uncommon for Habitat to construct communal toilets. "You pay a small fee each time you use the toilet," Steve says, "and that money goes to pay for an attendant whose job it is to keep the toilet clean and usable." Because of the

PEOPLE LIVING IN THE DEVELOPED WORLD generally take for granted that their homes will have numerous faucets out of which clean water always flows. In the developing world, however, indoor plumbing is a luxury. Here, residents of a shantytown on the outskirts of Lusaka, Zambia, draw water from a shared well.

high volume of waste in urban areas, urban toilets (whether indoor or communal) are typically connected to public sewer systems, which carry the waste to sewage treatment plants.

A s PART OF THE 1999 Carter Work Project in the Philippines, Valerie Bean and fourteen thousand other volunteers built 293 homes in five days. Each home had a flush toilet connected to a septic system. Next to each toilet was a water barrel, which homeowners filled by hand using buckets. After each use of the toilet, the homeowner would draw water from the barrel and use it to flush the toilet.

Bill and Stein Metzger on their Philippines trip

Father and son Bill and Stein Metzger also took part in that build. An inquisitive man, Bill began exploring the world in 1962, when he joined the Peace Corps. After serving in Venezuela for two years, he worked for another year and a half at the agency's Washington headquarters. There, he met his future wife, Melodee, a native of Honolulu. From 1965 until 1968, the Metzgers worked together in Chile before leaving the Peace Corps and moving to Honolulu, where Bill became a high school English teacher and Stein was born in 1972.

Meanwhile, Bill and Melodee became quite adept at home building. "Moving to expensive Honolulu on a teacher's salary was a bit daunting," Bill says. "We weren't able to afford a home of our own on Oahu, so we bought a couple of small building lots on the big island of Hawaii, where property was cheaper. We put up three houses over there, one per summer for three consecutive summers, and we did most of the work ourselves. I learned about foundations, framing, siding, and roofing, although I did have to hire out the electrical and the plumbing." Those homes turned out to be excellent investments. The value of each appreciated, and the Metzgers were soon able to afford a lot in Honolulu, where they built the house in which they still live.

Bill began building with Habitat in the early 1990s, volunteering on weekends and gradually working his way up to house leader. "I had some skills, and I had something to give," Bill says. "The main reason that I volunteer is that I've had a very blessed life. I've had a lot of things work out favorably for me and my family, and I just couldn't continue to accumulate all of these riches, in various forms, without lending a hand myself."

In 1998, after his retirement from teaching, Bill was working on a new investment property with Stein when he learned about the upcoming Carter Work Project in the Philippines. "The timing was right," Bill explains, "and the trip turned out to be a wonderful bonding experience. I signed both of us up as house leaders because I

What's It For? *Because composting toilets don't use water, they can be installed in houses without plumbing. The waste, instead of being flushed into a sewer or septic system, passes into a receiving tank, where it decomposes naturally.*

knew Stein had the construction skills and the leadership ability, and we got houses right next door to each other. In fact, the houses were so close that I could stand between them, reach out my arms, and touch both at the same time."

"We went to the Philippines after I had moved to California to go to college," Stein remembers, "so it was really nice to have the opportunity to reconnect with my dad as an adult." Bill and Stein roomed together and ate together, and if Stein had a question on the job site, Bill was always there to answer it. "To be together all day every day for two weeks is something that we've never been able to duplicate," Stein says regretfully.

By late afternoon on the last day of the build, both Bill and Stein were exhausted. As Stein recalls, "We had been told to get as far as we could but not to worry because some professionals would be coming in afterward to take care of whatever we couldn't finish. We worked our tails off that whole last day to finish what we could, but finally we got to a place where we were just so tired that we were ready to call it quits."

"It was five o'clock," Bill says, "and most people were just standing around, waiting to leave for dinner. My house wasn't done, but I was done and ready to go home. Then down the road comes President Carter. Wherever he went, he was the story, and people always wanted to take pictures with him and talk to him, but he was there to work. He was very focused on his own house, of course, but from time to time he would just take a walk and see how other people were doing.

"So he stops at my house and looks at me," Bill continues, "and says, 'How's it going?' And I say, 'Good.' And he says, 'You have your toilet in?' Well, until that moment, I'd been feeling pretty good about getting 95 percent of the work done, but my toilet wasn't in. 'No, sir,' I said. And then he said, 'If I show you how to put it in, will you help me?'

"I thought to myself, *Am I going to say no to the president?*" Bill chuckles. "So I said, 'Yes, sir!' And he said, 'Come with me.' So we go into the house, and in the corner, where the bathroom was going to be, there was a drain hole about four or five inches in diameter. The toilet was sitting there, and so was a bag of mortar. The president said, 'Mix up some of that mortar over there.' So I mixed some mortar. And he said, 'Let me have it, and now you watch.' Then he took the mortar and made a little circle a couple inches high around the drain hole. Next, he took the toilet and set it gently on the mortar. Finally, he took his level and leveled the toilet both ways. Seventy-five years old, and there he was on his hands and knees, setting that toilet! When he was done, he turned to me and said, 'That's the way you do it. Now go show your son.' I don't know how he knew that Stein was the house leader next door, but I said, 'Yes, sir,' and off he went."

President Carter adjusts a window on one of the houses built during the 1999 Philippines work project.

Benton Harbor, Michigan

Maragondon, Philippi

Asan, South Korea

Riga, Indones

Lonavala, India

Lilongwe, Mala

8. Transformation

SOMETIMES, the experience that you have on a Habitat job site can take you by surprise. You can be expecting one thing to happen, and instead something else does that changes your life forever. Certainly, that happened to more than a few people at the 2006 Carter Work Project in Lonavala, India.

As President Carter likes to point out, the Lonavala build took place not far from the town where his mother, Miss Lillian, spent her Peace Corps years. "It was a homecoming in a way," the president says. It was also the usual reunion. All the Kirks were there—including Dale, who agreed to serve as construction director and made four trips to India in the months leading up to the October blitz build. "Some business and personal issues forced me to come home prematurely," Dale says, "but I went back in the fall and was there for a few weeks before the build started."

As usual, Sherwood and Marsha worked on the Carter house, joined by Habitat CEO Jonathan Reckford and actor Brad Pitt.

HABITAT PARTNER FAMILIES CELEBRATE
THE COMPLETION OF THEIR HOMES.

"Brad showed up in India and worked his tail off," President Carter remembers. "So many people heard about it and wanted to work with him that we were inundated with volunteers and finished the houses in four days instead of the usual five."

Brad Pitt (right) and Habitat CEO Jonathan Reckford hoist a window into place.

An even bigger draw than Brad Pitt was Indian film star John Abraham. "It was funny, but it made sense," recalls Court Clayton, a national fundraiser for Habitat. "Brad Pitt is an American superstar, but there are only three hundred million Americans. John Abraham is an equally big star in India, and there are more than a billion Indians.

"All of the Indian volunteers were starstruck," Court continues, "and I remember that a homeowner at the Carter house was incredibly disappointed when he found out that John Abraham was working on someone else's house. He had Jimmy Carter and Brad Pitt but not John Abraham."

JOHN BECAME INVOLVED with Habitat when one of his closest friends asked him to meet with Joseph Scaria, then the director of Habitat India. "I said definitely," John remembers. "So I met Joseph, and I completely fell in love with his ideas and with Habitat for Humanity. The need for Habitat in a country like India is very great—and not only in India but also in Bangladesh, Pakistan, Sri Lanka, and Nepal. These are all countries that feed off Indian films, and I thought that, being an Indian film actor, I could provide a platform for Habitat in these areas. That was easy for me to do, and I saw an immediate response. People began saying they wanted to come and help, and I found that so beautiful."

According to John, one of his most memorable experiences at Lonavala was getting to meet Jimmy Carter. "It was really nice to meet this eighty-plus-year-old gentleman who comes over here and does such amazing work for our country. He is so full of energy that he actually leads by example. He's shown a lot of us here and around the world that we can do a lot if we have the inclination to do so. I think it's all about making the time to do good work."

As John was finishing up his work at Lonavala, Joseph Scaria let him know that the elderly woman on whose house he had been working wanted to thank him personally.

"A seventy-year-old lady came up to me," John says. "Her hands were folded, and she was smiling, and that's when it really hit me as to what I had done. I kid you not. It didn't affect me before then so much as after, and that realization gave me the impetus to go on. For example, I was told that there was

Everybody is equal on a Habitat site. The only hierarchy is height: if you're working on the roof, then you're at a high level; if you're laying tiles in the bathroom, then you're at a low level. But that's the only difference. No one is big or small in terms of stature or society. We're all the same because we're all there for a common cause: to build homes for the needy. —John Abraham

John Abraham shares a joke during a break at Lonavala.

a five-million-dollar check for Habitat for Humanity waiting in Dubai, but they wouldn't release it unless I made an appearance. I told them I would go, but I said I was also going to beg for more money. So I went to Dubai. I got the five million dollars, and while I was there, I auctioned off a lot of my stuff—a jacket, a T-shirt, and so on—and made nearly another million dollars. That's the really beautiful thing about Habitat. It makes you realize that you need to do things for other people. Unfortunately, there aren't enough people yet who've come to see that, so we need to go out and touch a lot more hearts."

YOUNG ZUNAIRA HIJAZI didn't draw the same crowds as Brad Pitt and John Abraham, but she and the seven other Seeds of Peace who took part in the Lonavala build did become, as Court Clayton says, "mini-celebrities." The reason was that Zunaira is Pakistani, and most Indians consider Pakistanis to be their enemies.

The Seeds of Peace program was founded in 1993 by John Wallach, a journalist who wanted to empower exceptional young people from regions of conflict throughout the world. Wallach's goal was to teach leadership skills to fourteen- and fifteen-year-olds so that, as they got older, they could advocate for reconciliation and peace within their own countries. Wallach began the program by inviting forty-six teenagers from Israel, Palestine, and Egypt to spend three weeks at a summer camp in Otisfield, Maine. There, in addition to the usual sports and recreation activities, the Seeds would take part in conflict-resolution and coexistence workshops designed to promote interaction and understanding.

Three of the Seeds of Peace — (from left to right) Akanksha Gandhi, Zunaira Hijazi, and Sasha Mansukhani — pose for a photo with their crew leader at Lonavala.

In 2001, with financial support from the U.S. State Department, the Seeds of Peace program was expanded to include teenagers from South Asia. Each year, program officials from India, a predominantly Hindu country, and Pakistan, a predominantly Muslim country, conduct a rigorous selection process to identify new Seeds. Following a series of school recommendations, essays, and interviews, these officials narrow the field of applicants down to twenty-four students—six boys and six girls from each country—who are then sent to Maine to begin the Seeds experience.

"The program creates an opportunity for teenagers from both sides to come to a neutral place and talk about their differences," explains Sajjad Ahmad, the director of the Seeds program in Pakistan. "John Wallach understood that today's teenagers are tomorrow's leaders. If we can sow the seeds of peace in them, we

RECOGNIZING THAT most poor people in the world build their homes incrementally — a room at a time as money becomes available — Habitat has begun working with local organizations to provide microfinancing (small, short-term loans) for badly needed improvements. "We understand that not everybody can meet the water and sanitation standards," explains Habitat's Steve Weir, "but what a great thing to pour a permanent concrete floor and then to be able to add a ceiling so that the floor stays dry." In this photograph, an Indian woman holds up the bankbook for her microfinance account.

can hopefully look forward to peace in the future. At camp, these so-called enemies learn to work together and become teammates."

After the Seeds return from Maine, they enter extensive follow-up programs run by Sajjad and his Indian counterpart, Feruzan Mehta. Sajjad and Feruzan keep the Seeds engaged by helping them organize monthly meetings, regional conferences, and home stays, in which Indian Seeds visit the homes of Pakistani Seeds and vice versa.

Zunaira was in ninth grade when Seeds of Peace selected her to become part of the first Pakistani delegation. "I was very excited because it was going to be my first trip to the United States," she says. "But I was also apprehensive because I would be meeting the 'enemy,' and I didn't know what would happen. I'd never seen an Indian before, and I had a lot of mixed emotions."

The negative emotions disappeared as soon as Zunaira arrived in camp. "It was awesome," she says. "Now that I look back on it,

I can see that it was the best experience of my life. For three weeks, we ate together, had activities together, talked about the conflict together—basically, we coexisted—and I took all of that back with me. Now I knew a little bit about people on the other side, and I wanted to make people on my side understand what I had learned."

THE PARTNERSHIP between Seeds of Peace and Habitat for Humanity came about because of a personal connection between Habitat's Court Clayton and Tom Hancock, who was then the director of the Seeds of Peace South Asia program. Tom's wife, Holly, an enthusiastic Habitat volunteer, had already taken part in the 2004 Carter Work Project in Puebla, Mexico; and at her suggestion, Tom invited Court up to Maine to learn more about Seeds of Peace.

Court's visit to the Otisfield camp took place in July 2006, about three months before the Lonavala build. "As I learned more about the camp and what Tom was doing, it seemed like a natural fit to get some of these Seeds involved with the Carter project," Court says. "So I was the one who floated the idea, but the real credit belongs to Tom and Holly, who actually made the partnership happen."

Although Habitat affiliates have varying guidelines for how old a volunteer needs to be to participate, the Carter Work Project requires that volunteers be at least eighteen years old. Because none of the current Seeds were old enough, Feruzan and Sajjad began surveying Seeds from 2001 and 2002, which is how Zunaira found her way to Lonavala. Getting there wasn't easy, however, because of the political tension that exists between India and Pakistan. Obtaining governmental approval for the home stays had always been "very problematic," Tom Hancock remembers, and even when permission was granted, it was also sometimes revoked. "We didn't know whether the Seeds from Pakistan were going to be allowed into India until literally the day before the build," Court says. But the visas finally came through, and the Pakistani Seeds got on the next available plane.

Court Clayton with Pakistani Seed Zunaira Hijazi (left) and Indian Seed Parinaz Vakil

"The Indian volunteers were very interested in the Pakistani Seeds," Court remembers. "For most of them, it was probably the first time they had ever seen a Pakistani in person. But watching the Pakistani Seeds work so hard and so diligently really made a lasting impression on the Indians who were there."

Sasha Mansukhani, one of the four Indian Seeds at Lonavala, was especially happy to see her friend Zunaira again. "It's not very easy to get her down from Pakistan," Sasha says. "And I was so glad that we got a chance to work with each other and show the Indians here—say, the person whose house we were working on—what Pakistanis are really like. I mean, most Indians have never met a Pakistani, and now this lady has actually seen one working on her house, and she's never going to have a stereotype about a Pakistani again. She's never going to think that they're bad people, which is what our media often wants us to believe."

Of course, for the Seeds themselves, the idea of Indians and Pakistanis working together was nothing new. Several years had already passed since their camp experiences; and through the follow-up programs, especially the home stays, many had become close friends. "What Tom really wanted the Seeds to get out of their Habitat experience," Court explains, "was the idea of service, especially service to members of a lower caste, or social class. The kids who are selected to take part in the Seeds program are the best students from the best schools. That's why they're expected to become leaders later in life. It's also why many of them come from privileged backgrounds. They haven't had much interaction with poor people, and I don't know that any of them has done much volunteering to help the sort of people who work as servants in their parents' homes. But at Lonavala, all of a sudden, that barrier of class came falling down for these kids, and it was incredible to see."

For most of the Seeds, performing manual labor was an entirely new experience. "I'd never done anything like that before," Zunaira says. "Back home, we have a cook, we have a driver, and we don't do labor-intensive work. So before I got to Lonavala, I wondered how in the world I was going to build a house. How was I even going to *help* build a house? But the house leader gave us each a helmet [hard hat] and showed us what to do, and we started right off mixing the mortar. The next day, we painted nearly the entire house, and I'd never painted before. It was very easy and interesting at first, but then it got very tiring, and I said to myself, *Oh, my God, this is a lot of work!* I remember thinking about all the people who build houses every day—the people who must have built my house—and how we take their work for granted. I don't do that anymore."

What's It For? *Habitat volunteers use an average of fifty gallons of paint to cover an entire three-bedroom house.*

Another of the Indian Seeds who worked alongside Zunaira at Lonavala was Akanksha Gandhi. "Somehow, everyone forgot who they were and set their own lives aside to come together and build the houses," Akanksha explains. "My clearest memory comes from the second day, when I was painting one of the doors to the house, and the lady who was going to be the homeowner was sitting beside me. I asked her, 'Do you like what we've done so far?' And she started to cry and said, 'It's the most beautiful thing that has ever happened to me in my life.' That memory is something I'll take with me for the rest of my life."

THE HUNDRED HOMES built at Lonavala were all duplexes—single structures containing two living units, or apartments. At the Carter duplex, Habitat CEO Jonathan Reckford worked closely not only with Brad Pitt but also with the two partner families—Sadhiya and Aziz Sheikh, who are Muslim, and Shalini and Subhash Sathe, who are Hindu. That the Sheikh and Sathe families were going to be neighbors was unusual in India, where members of different religions tend to live apart. But, as Jonathan Reckford explains, the Habitat process brought these two families together. "It was a wonderful example of how Habitat can be a bridge builder," he says. "I'll never forget how, at the dedication of the two homes, Subhash put his arm around his new neighbor, Aziz, and said, 'You know, we're from different faiths—I'm Hindu, and he's Muslim—and we're from different castes'—which in India can be a significant social barrier—'but now we're brothers.'"

Aziz Sheikh (left) and Subhash Sathe at the joint dedication of their new Habitat homes

Marsha and Sherwood Kirk embrace a tearful Shalini Sathe during the joint house dedication.

At the time, Subhash's wife, Shalini, was pregnant and "due any minute," according to Marsha Kirk. "So I was just protective of her all week. Every morning, we'd say a Christian prayer, a Hindu prayer, a Muslim prayer, and then go to work. Neither of us could speak the other's language, but we formed a bond anyway, and when Sherwood and I got ready to leave at the end of the week, she just clung to me, bawling."

This sort of thing happens all the time to Sherwood and Marsha, but they never get tired of it or take it for granted. "One time in— I forget the country, might have been Northern Ireland—I was talking with this fellow who said, 'So, Kirk, you enjoy them sending you over here, don't you?' I said, 'What do you mean, *sending me over*? Habitat doesn't pay me.' And he said, 'Oh, well, they don't pay you, I know, but they give you a plane ticket.' And I said, 'No, I have to pay for my own plane ticket.' And he said, 'Well, yeah, you pay for your own plane ticket, but they give you a place to stay.' And I said, 'No, Habitat volunteers have to pay all of their own expenses and also make a donation.' That really puzzled him, and he said, 'Wait a minute, Kirk. You're telling me you pay *your own way* to come here to work on these houses. I don't understand.'" So Sherwood explained to this man the reason that he and Marsha and Dale and Valerie Bean and Kraig Koschnick and Wendy Gabry and Tom Gerdy and Bill and Stein Metzger and more than one million other people, including Jimmy and Rosalynn Carter, volunteer for Habitat.

"People are people," Sherwood says, "and when you go to these foreign countries and different places to build with Habitat, you find out that the people there are just like you. They want a place to lay their head. They want their kids to have an education. They just want the same things that we all want, and it's really brought out when you go and get involved in their lives enough to build them a home.

"I've got to say one thing, though," he continues, choking up with emotion. "The partner families all say, 'Thank you, thank you, thank you for coming to build our home.' But I want to say"—and Sherwood pauses here, fighting back tears—"thanks for letting us do it. I just want to thank them for letting us come to build their home. I mean, they're letting us *build their home,* and we're getting so much more out of it than they are."

I think that everybody who comes to work with Habitat comes out of a religious commitment to do something good for somebody else. It has been especially interesting for me to see the relationships that develop between people of different religions. You realize just how much you have in common, how many of your thoughts are similar.
—Rosalynn Carter

China

Laos

Cambodia

Vietnam

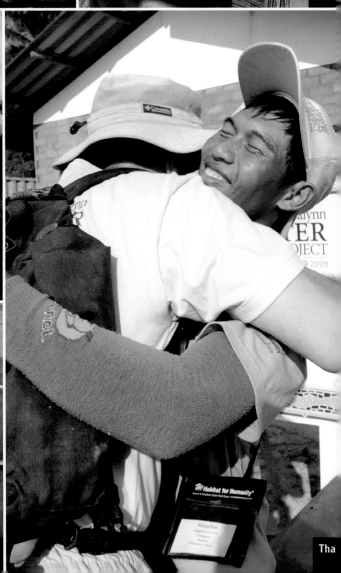
Tha

Postscript

BEFORE I BEGAN writing this book, I knew that I had a choice to make. I had to decide whether or not to participate in a Habitat build as part of my research. I decided not to, because I was worried that if I did, I might—without knowing it—reshape the stories other people told me in order to fit my own experience.

I waited to build but not for long. As soon as I finished writing the manuscript, my wife, Julia, and I signed up for the 2009 Jimmy and Rosalynn Carter Work Project. We were eager to begin but also a little intimidated, because the work project was taking place halfway around the world. Called the Mekong Build, it spanned five sites in Southeast Asian countries through which the Mekong River flows. Julia and I chose the main build site in Chiang Mai, Thailand, because that was where many of the people I had interviewed for the book would be working.

Making our travel plans was tricky. Because there are no direct flights from the United States to Chiang Mai, we had to stop off in

SCENES FROM THE FIVE BUILD SITES THAT MADE UP THE 2009 JIMMY AND ROSALYNN CARTER WORK PROJECT

Seoul, South Korea, to change planes. The flights were so long that it took us twenty-four hours to reach our destination. By the time we got there, we were exhausted.

As it turned out, our flight from Seoul to Chiang Mai had a lot of Habitat volunteers onboard, including President and Mrs. Carter. The plane left Seoul at 8:50 P.M. local time, but it felt like six in the morning to our bodies, which were still on New York time — and we hadn't slept all night!

I'm sure the other Americans on the plane were feeling equally tired. Yet shortly before takeoff, President Carter roused himself from his seat and walked up and down the entire length of the airplane, shaking hands and thanking everyone for volunteering. A Korean businessman sitting beside me noticed the commotion and, realizing that the man coming down the aisle must be important, turned to me and asked, "George Bush?" "No," I replied, "Jimmy Carter." "Ah!" he said, and smiled.

ARRIVING IN CHIANG MAI late on a Friday night, Julia and I checked into our hotel and went to sleep right away. On Saturday and Sunday, we did a little sightseeing, but mostly we rested because we knew that the build would be starting very early Monday morning.

Every day, we had the same schedule: wake up at 4:30 A.M., eat breakfast in the hotel at 5:00 A.M., board the buses for the job site at 6:00 A.M., and start work by 7:00 A.M. Except for a brief lunch break, we worked until 5:00 P.M., then boarded the buses again for the trip back to the hotel. We arrived at the hotel around 6:00 P.M.

This is how the Chiang Mai site looked when the volunteers arrived. Local workers had already poured the cement floors and laid the first eight courses of blocks.

filthy with cement dust, mortar, and sweat. After cleaning up, we ate dinner about 7:00 P.M.

Besides Julia and me, the Habitat staff had to take care of two thousand other volunteers in Chiang Mai, which was quite an undertaking. Their efforts made it possible for us to focus on our work and build an entire neighborhood of eighty-two houses in just five days. (The number of homes was chosen to honor the king of Thailand, who was about to celebrate his eighty-second birthday.)

There were three main construction tasks. The first was laying the interlocking blocks that made up the walls of each house. These blocks are an inexpensive building material made out of cement and soil. They look like oversize LEGOs, and they're almost as easy to build with, because rounded bumps on the tops match rounded indentations on the bottoms.

An important difference between interlocking blocks and LEGOs, however, is that merely stacking the blocks isn't enough to hold them together, at least not permanently. To make the walls of the house rigid and strong, we had to fill holes in the blocks with a mortar made of small rocks (called aggregate) and cement. Filling these holes was the second main task.

Actress Emily Bergl and martial arts film star Jet Li work with interlocking blocks on House #40.

Because of the way the interlocking blocks are designed, the holes in them line up. So the mortar that we poured down the holes ran through all the courses, or layers, of block to the house's poured cement floor. When the mortar dried, it formed concrete columns that held the blocks together. Nothing could budge them.

The third main task was filling the gaps between blocks on the inside and outside faces of the walls. For this work, called pointing, we used a smoother mortar, made of sand and cement instead of aggregate and cement. We were taught that the proper way to point a wall was for one worker to fill a small plastic bag with sand mortar and squeeze it into the joints in the same way that a baker squeezes icing from a pastry bag onto a cake. Once several joints were filled, another worker scraped off the excess and sponged the wall clean.

J ULIA AND I worked on House #2. Many of the other houses were being built by crews made up of people who knew one another before they got to Chiang Mai. Some were employees of the same sponsor company; others belonged to the same Habitat affiliate. Because these people were already familiar with one another, they communicated easily and worked efficiently.

Our house, on the other hand, had a crew made up of people who hadn't known one another before the build. In all, there were five Americans and ten Thais. The Americans, besides Julia and me, included our house leader, Jim, and another married couple, Gregg and DeAnna. The ten Thais included five women from Amway Thailand, a major sponsor of the build; two border patrolmen; two men from the same factory, one the head of a maintenance crew and the other an assembly-line supervisor; and, of course, the homeowner.

An immediate concern was language. The Americans spoke no Thai, and the Thai men spoke little or no English. The Amway ladies spoke some English — enough to translate the occasional question, such as "Have you seen the rubber mallet lately?"—but we struggled time and again to communicate, which made the difficult work that much harder. What I didn't realize at the time was that if the work had been easier, the experience wouldn't have meant so much to me.

What's It For? *This pointing tool is used to clean up recently filled joints. Dragging its tip along the groove between two interlocking blocks scrapes away excess mortar.*

ALL EIGHTY-TWO HOMES being built in Chiang Mai had identical building plans. They were all built out of identical materials using identical tools. But don't let that fool you: there are still many ways to build a house.

First thing Monday, the Americans working on House #2 got together to make a plan. We asked ourselves some key questions: What had to be accomplished that day? What resources did we have? How should those resources, such as manpower and tools, be deployed?

I could tell that the Amway ladies were especially eager to get going, but they waited patiently for our conference to end and for Jim, our house leader, to show them what to do. The Thai men, whose lack of English made it difficult for them to understand what was happening, didn't wait. They simply went to work, laying courses of blocks at the back of the house.

The proper way to do this, Jim explained, was to lay one course at a time all the way around the house, using a string line to make sure that the walls were straight before moving on to the next course. The Thai men decided to use a different method; and by the time we Americans finished making our plan, they had already put up half of the back wall. I could see that they were using a string and carefully tapping blocks into alignment, but they certainly weren't on board with the one-course-at-a-time plan.

Jim, who was not sure what else to do, put the Amway ladies to work pouring mortar down holes and pointing blocks, while Julia, Gregg, DeAnna, and I went to work on the front walls. That's how we spent the first two days: our house's three constituencies worked not at cross purposes but also not as a team.

Members of the House #2 crew on Tuesday. David is in the middle with the red shirt. Julia is in the back row on the far left. The Amway volunteeers are wearing light green shirts.

Working that way left everyone feeling a little frustrated. We were all motivated to work hard and do a good job, but language and cultural barriers were keeping us apart, and we hadn't yet figured out how to overcome them. The Amway ladies did their best to bridge the gap, especially engaging the American women; but the Thai men and the American men continued to work separately. Our lack of teamwork meant that we weren't working as effectively as we could have, nor were we having as much fun as we might have had.

THE WORK SCHEDULE called for us to finish the walls on Tuesday, but we fell a little behind and didn't get them done until Wednesday morning. After we laid the last course, we installed the brackets that would anchor the roof trusses to the walls. The brackets were set in cement, which had to dry before we could attach the trusses. Otherwise, the weight of the trusses would shift the brackets out of alignment.

The rear roof truss being hoisted into place

Raising the three roof trusses was a big deal. Each measured twenty-five feet in length and weighed more than 350 pounds, so they were difficult to work with and a little scary, too, because we had to lift them ten feet off the ground by hand. To get this difficult job done, everyone would have to work together. There was no other choice.

While waiting for the bracket cement to set, our crew took a rest break in the shade at the back of the house. Although everyone continued to smile and behave politely to one another, people seemed a little nervous about raising the trusses. One reason, I think, was that some of the missteps we had made on Monday and Tuesday — nothing serious, but a few that were noticeable — had undermined the Thais' confidence.

This feeling was confirmed to me when Wanida, one of the Amway ladies, took me aside and asked me with some concern in her voice, "Do you have a manual for this?" The trusses looked awfully heavy to her, and she wanted some reassurance that we weren't making things up as we went along. I wasn't sure what to tell her because, for my part, I *was* figuring things out as I went along. But she felt better when Gregg and I went next door to watch another crew put up its trusses. We asked a lot of questions; and when we came back, Wanida translated what we had learned for the benefit of the Thai men. Then everybody got ready to lift the trusses.

Before Wednesday afternoon, I knew the first name of only one of the four Thai men. One reason was that many Thais go by a nickname that has no relation to their given name. For example, our homeowner's given name was Chanida, which is what Habitat printed on her name tag. But the other Thais all referred to her using her nickname, which was Jasmin. For several days, I thought Chanida and Jasmin were two different people, and I had similar problems with the men's names. But by the time we had lifted the trusses and bolted them into place, I knew all of the men's names, and they knew mine. Working together made that happen.

Once the trusses were up, we began hoisting and bolting the purlins into place. Purlins are horizontal bars that span the trusses and tie the roof frame together. Like the trusses, they're heavy; and lifting them in the hot sun left us all very tired. When we were done, we all congratulated one another and took a break.

There was just one small problem: we had neglected to attach the two spacer bars that link the bottom of the middle truss to the bottoms of the front and rear trusses, respectively. These spacers were supposed to be installed before the purlins went up — while the trusses still had some give — but we had goofed. When I tried to install the spacers after the purlins were bolted down, I found that one of them wouldn't reach from the rear truss to the middle truss. There was a four-inch gap between the bolt hole in the truss and the bolt hole in the spacer.

We immediately fetched one of the block leaders, who supervises the house leaders, and he told us that we would have to take down all eight purlins in order to put some flex back into the trusses. The thought of having to undo all our hard work and start over was highly demoralizing — but then our team rallied.

Bert, the assembly-line supervisor, quietly climbed onto the middle truss and began pulling the spacer toward him. Then

Bert (left) and Jack install roof tiles. The J-bolts sticking up through the tiles hook on to the purlins underneath.

Jack, one of the border patrolmen, noticed what Bert was doing, climbed onto the rear truss, and began tugging the spacer from the other end. DeAnna was standing on some scaffolding beneath the middle truss. She had been listening carefully to the block leader, but then she looked up, saw what Bert and Jack were doing, and called out in surprise, "Oh! Wait! Just a little more . . . *there*!" And she pushed the bolt through the truss into the spacer.

Somehow, Bert, who is quite a bit smaller than I am, had mustered the superhuman strength necessary to pull the roof together nearly by himself. Jack had helped, of course, but the feat was still remarkable. I was so elated and so impressed that I yelled out, "Superman!"

Bert doesn't speak English. Even so, he understood what I had said because Superman is an international hero. Immediately, his face broke out in a big smile, and so did the faces of everyone else on our crew, not only because we wouldn't have to take down the purlins but also because it felt like we'd finally become a team.

FROM THAT POINT ON, everyone worked together much more closely, and we had a lot more fun. We spent Thursday installing the cement tiles that covered the roof and moving ahead with the pointing. The only item on my personal to-do list that I hadn't ticked off yet was getting to know the homeowner.

For most of the week, I wasn't sure how to relate to Jasmin. I'd heard plenty of stories from Sherwood and Marsha Kirk and Valerie Bean about the bonds that form between partner families and volunteers; and President Carter had explained to me very clearly that the point of Habitat, as far as he was concerned, was to bridge the chasm between the haves (me) and the have-nots (Jasmin). So by the end of the day on Thursday, I was feeling a little guilty that I hadn't yet bridged that chasm myself.

Even so, I knew that I couldn't force a relationship, nor should I try, because to do so would be patronizing. Instead, I interacted with Jasmin in the same way that I did with everyone else: Can you help me with this? Can I help you with that? She probably felt equally uncertain. After all, this was her first Habitat build, too.

On Friday afternoon, however, with about two hours of work left until the dedication ceremony, I took a tumble and dislocated the middle joint of my pinkie finger. Not a big deal, but I had to go to the medical tent and get a temporary splint, which meant no more lifting for me. When I got back to the house, Julia told me that plants for the yard had just arrived and that they needed to be put in the ground right away. She said that I should take care of this after finding out from Jasmin where the plants should go.

With the help of a translator, I consulted Jasmin; and she replied that she wanted me to choose, because that would be "a symbol of good health." I wasn't sure what she meant, but the impression I got was that she thought it would be good luck for me to decide on the locations. I said that I would but I first wanted to take a walk around the block to see what other house crews were doing. Wanida suggested that Jasmin accompany me and help with the planting because of the splint on my hand.

David and Jasmin plant a mango tree in front of Jasmin's new home.

Jasmin and I had fun on our walk. She managed to explain to me the growing habits of the plants — *big, not so big* — and, because I'm a gardener at home, I was able to come up with a landscape design that she liked. As I watched her digging the holes for the plants and watering them in, I could sense that her dream of home ownership was finally becoming a reality, and I was thrilled to be a part of that process.

LATER, on the final bus ride back to the hotel, Julia remarked that the work project reminded her of summer camp, and I think she's right. Like young summer campers, adult volunteers leave their daily lives behind to spend a week in the company of like-minded people.

David eating lunch with President Carter (wearing a red bandanna) and hundreds of other volunteers

We eat together; we bunk together; we travel from place to place together. Everything is provided for us so that we can focus entirely on the work at hand.

Also like summer campers, we want the experience to last as long as possible, because we know that we'll miss it when we're done and we step back into our home and work lives. We'll long for the brief opportunity we were given to be a different kind of adult.

That we were able to reinvent ourselves seems fitting because, in a larger sense, the Carter Work Project reinvented our world. For those five days in Chiang Mai, Thai and foreign volunteers alike lived and worked together in a world characterized by cooperation, generosity, kindness, and compassion. Who wouldn't want to keep such a world alive? Who wouldn't want to return to it year after year, as so many volunteers do?

Much came into focus for me during President Carter's closing remarks. As at the opening ceremonies, the president was greeted with a loud and lengthy standing ovation, conveying the personal devotion that so many Habitat volunteers feel toward him and Mrs. Carter. When they applauded President Carter, they were not merely acknowledging what he and Mrs. Carter have done for other people; they were also showing their appreciation for what the Carters have done for *them*, specifically by creating a meaningful way in which volunteers can share in Habitat's work of transformation.

I've been back home for a couple of weeks now; and, of course, the exhilaration has faded, especially as the gravitational pull of doctor's appointments and parent-teacher conferences and family dinners has reestablished itself. But there is one part of my Chiang Mai experience that I know won't fade, because so many Habitat volunteers have told me that it doesn't.

During the week that I spent in Chiang Mai, the world in which I lived was a different place, a better place. Having experienced that in real time made an indelible impression on me. I'm in no position to tell you whether what happened in Chiang Mai can be repeated or extended beyond the next Carter Work Project, but I can tell you this with assurance: better *is* possible. You just have to be open to the possibilities.

The Chiang Mai build site at the end of the work project on Friday. The local workers who prepared the site will finish whatever tasks remain to be done.

Afterword

by Jonathan Reckford

Christ has no body now but yours,
No hands, no feet on earth but yours.

—Saint Teresa of Ávila

ONE OF THE INTERESTING THINGS we learn as we grow older is how the world can be both big and small all at the same time. That's a bit of a riddle and a contradiction, to be sure, but even with billions of people in hundreds of countries speaking many diverse languages, it turns out that people are more similar than we are different.

We all have a need for food and shelter, and we all want to take care of our families and friends and live lives of dignity. But for low-income families in the United States and around the world, satisfying these basic human needs can be a significant hardship. The work of Habitat for Humanity is to offer families who find themselves in challenging situations the opportunity for a better life.

Although you may not realize it, you have the ability to change the lives of families like these for the better. It's an awesome ability that most people don't realize they possess. They see all the troubles and challenges in the world and quickly become overwhelmed. They don't see how to solve a problem or even where to start. Some throw their hands up in frustration. Others sit on their hands and hope someone else figures things out. Neither strategy is effective or productive. The truth is, as Saint Teresa of Ávila said, that when it comes to solving problems and making a difference in the world, *there are no hands on earth but yours.*

This book tells the story of how Habitat for Humanity, using Christian principles, has taken the simple idea of helping people live in safe, decent homes and turned it into a global ministry that has sheltered more than one million people. Just as important, all the work has been done by ordinary people like you who decided that they wanted to make a difference.

I am always amazed at the tireless dedication of the Habitat faithful—not least our most famous volunteers, Jimmy and Rosalynn Carter. Their work, enthusiasm, and commitment to helping the world's less fortunate set an example for us all. The former president and First Lady have done more for this ministry than they, or we, can ever know, and yet in their modesty they are reluctant to accept credit.

"We have become small players in an exciting global effort to alleviate the curse of homelessness," President Carter has said. "With our many new friends, we have worked to raise funds, to publicize the good work of Habitat, to recruit other volunteers, to visit overseas projects, and even to build a few houses."

In a quarter century of building with Habitat for Humanity, President and Mrs. Carter have certainly helped to erect more than a "few" houses. Meanwhile, in doing so, they have inspired countless other volunteers to join the effort, extending the reach of Habitat to many more families.

I am hopeful that through this book you, too, will be inspired by the Carters and the hard work of Habitat's many volunteers, supporters, and partner families. The future of Habitat for Humanity rests in your hands. So what will you do? Will you throw your hands up in the air? Sit on them and wait for others to act? Or use your hands to pick up a hammer or a shovel — or to raise awareness and funds so that the work can continue? Your choice of tool makes no difference, but choosing to pick one up can make all the difference in the world.

The world is not as big as it seems, and we can make it smaller still by choosing to get involved and help one another. Remember, there are no hands but yours.

Jonathan Reckford is the chief executive officer of Habitat for Humanity International.

Acknowledgments

As with a Habitat house, it takes many hands to make a book, and all deserve recognition. I should begin by thanking President and Mrs. Carter, whose support for this project—as well as for the work of Habitat—has been generous, inspirational, and steadfast. I would also like to thank the many Habitat homeowners and volunteers who, like the Carters, shared their personal experiences with me so that I might present them here. Most of their names are already familiar to you, because their words are quoted extensively throughout these pages. There are, however, several exceptions—Wale Adelowo, Shawn Means, Feruzan Mehta, and Tammy Stines—whose recollections provided useful background information.

The leadership and staff at Habitat for Humanity International also deserve special thanks. Rarely does an author have the opportunity to work with such a conscientious and capable group of people, and I'll miss my interactions with them. Bob Longino and Judy Lawrence provided me with hard-to-get contact information; and Karen Haycox, Antônio Prais, and Joseph Scaria helped me obtain hard-to-get interviews. Bob Jacob and Jennifer Graves helped the book's designer, Jon Glick, and me navigate Habitat's fabulous photo archive and shot for us images that weren't there. Jessica Boatright, Duane Bates, Donald Bonin, and Shala Carlson guided me through Habitat's many hallways; and Larry Perrault showed me around Habitat's Global Village & Discovery Center. Jill Claflin and Clive Rainey took me to a memorable lunch at Koinonia Farm, and Myra Hardy made sure that Jon and I were otherwise well fed during our stay in Americus.

Finally, I would like to thank my editor at Candlewick, Karen Lotz, for her infectious enthusiasm; Karen's assistant, Nicole Raymond, for briskly attending to my many requests; my agent, Amy Hughes, for her keen understanding of human nature; my wife, Julia, for her forbearance; and my children, Abigail and Quentin, who gave this book a beneficial first read. Julia and I often joke that we won't allow them to grow up any more. Only now do I realize the professional disadvantage I will suffer as an author of children's books when my own children graduate from middle school.

Postscript: For this new paperback edition, further thanks are due to the many Habitat staff members who made the 2009 Carter Work Project such a beneficial experience for me and thousands of others volunteers. At the top of that list is project manager Jennifer Lindsey. I would also like to single out Rita Bennett, who made sure that I and many others had a place to stay. Meanwhile, at Candlewick, Hilary Van Dusen oversaw the creation of this new edition with graciousness and a steady hand.

Index

Photo Credits

Habitat for Humanity International (HFHI): xii (bottom left), 3, 6, 7, 8, 9, 10, 18, 20, 22, 44, 138 (top right)

HFHI/Robert Baker: 114 (top center)

HFHI/Robert Burge: 24 (bottom right)

HFHI/Doral Chenoweth III: 58 (middle left and bottom right), 114 (top left)

HFHI/Will Crocker: 58 (top right), 94 (left bottom, right second from top, and right third from top)

HFHI/John Curry: 75, 81

HFHI/Mikel Flamm: 39, 59, 61, 114 (bottom left top and bottom left bottom), 117, 124 (middle left), 138 (middle left)

HFHI/Linda Fuller: xii (top left and top right), 17

HFHI/Susan Goldman: 112

HFHI/Steffan Hacker: 24 (top left, top right, and middle right), 42 (top left, middle left, and middle bottom right), 47, 71, 72 (top left and center right), 77, 82 (top), 94 (left top and center bottom), 95, 96 (top right), 98, 114 (top right), 127, 138 (top left)

HFHI/Don Hall: 96 (middle left)

HFHI/George Hipple: 58 (middle right), 126

HFHI/Lenny Jordan: 4, 5

HFHI/Bob Jacob: 1, 21, 43, 54 (top), 73, 86, 125, 133

HFHI/Julie Lopez: xii (bottom right), 14, 96 (top left)

HFHI/Kim MacDonald: 24 (middle left and bottom left), 29, 42 (top right, middle top right, and bottom right), 48, 58 (top left and bottom left), 64 (top left, top right top, and top right bottom), 72 (top right), 79 (aerial view), 96 (bottom right), 100, 114 (middle left and bottom right), 118, 123, 124 (middle right and bottom right), 130

HFHI/Joe Matthews: 24 (middle center)

HFHI/Chris McGranahan: 82 (bottom right), 110

HFHI/Ezra Millstein: 32, 53, 54 (bottom), 55, 56, 68, 94 (center top and right top), 138 (bottom left)

HFHI/Brian Myrick: 87, 92, 154

HFHI/Andy Nelson: 138 (bottom right), 139, 141, 143, 153

HFHI/Gregg Pachkowski: iv, viii, 64 (bottom), 72 (bottom right), 78-79 (sequence), 84, 96 (middle center, middle right, and bottom left), 107, 113, 124 (top left and bottom left), 129, 132, 135, 136, 142

HFHI/Alysia Peyton: 82 (bottom left)

HFHI/ Emil Popa: 99

HFHI/Michael A. Schwarz: 42 (bottom left), 72 (bottom left)

HFHI/Karen E. Segrave: 94 (right bottom)

HFHI/Bill Sitterly: 51 (right)

HFHI/Wendy Veney: 88 (both)

HFHI/Al Vitiello: 51 (left)

HFHI/Alicia Wagner: 114 (middle right), 124 (top right)

Valerie Bean: 106, 108

Wendy Gabry: 66

Jon Glick: xi, 25 (top), 35, 97, 102

Habitat for Humanity of Kanawha and Putnam County: 37, 41

Habitat for Humanity of Kent County: 62

Debbie Kinder: 25 (bottom), 26 (both), 36

Sherwood and Marsha Kirk: 104

Kraig Koschnick: 70

Bill Metzger: 120

Kat Narvaez: 67

Julia Rubel: 145, 146, 148, 151, 152

Weir Family: 60

How to Get Involved

Now that you have read about Habitat for Humanity, there are many ways to get involved. No matter how old you are, Habitat welcomes your interest and support.

Volunteer work on active build sites can begin for young people ages 16–18. For younger volunteers, there are many other ways to support Habitat's work.

Learn more!

There are a lot of games, activities, and resources available to help you find out more about poverty housing and how you can make a difference. Visit www.habitatyouthprograms.org to learn more.

Spread the word!

Share this book with your friends and family and tell them about the work that Habitat for Humanity is doing. Visit www.habitat.org for more information on Habitat's work around the world.

Volunteer!

You can make a difference. You might:

- Join a Youth United group in your area. Youth United brings young people ages 5–25 together to fund and build a Habitat house with their local affiliate.

- Organize a fundraiser at your school or church.

- Serve lunch or hand out water to Habitat volunteers.

Contact the Habitat for Humanity affiliate in your community to find out more about how you can help or to learn about Habitat youth programs in your area. You can find the affiliate nearest you at www.habitat.org/local.